Lawn Care Excellence

The Ultimate Guide to Cultivating and Maintaining a Lush Lawn Like a Professional

JAMIE TUKEY

Jamie Tukey

Table of Contents

Jamie Tukey

Book Introduction:

A thick, lush, green lawn—it's the dream, right? That carpet-like grass you want to walk through barefoot on a warm summer day. But let's get real: a beautiful lawn doesn't just happen. It takes work. And knowledge. And the right tools. And time. OK, it takes a lot. But it's so worth it when you look out your window and see that sea of green grass that makes your neighbors jealous.

That's where this book comes in. It willprovide everything you need to grow and maintain the lawn of your dreams. We'll start with the basics, like understanding your lawn's needs. What kind of grass you have. How much sun does it get? What's your soil like? We'll get into things such as mowing, watering, fertilizing—all the fundamentals of lawn care.

But we're not stopping there. We'll also dive into more advanced techniques, like soil testing, weed and pest control, and disease prevention. We'lll walk you through how to care for your lawn during every season—spring, summer, fall, and winter—so you can have the lushest, healthiest grass year-round.

We'll also talk about tools and equipment. You might think you only need a mower, but we'll look at other necessary equipment like aerators, dethatchers, sprinklers, and more. We'll offer tips on choosing what's right for your lawn and budget.

If you're interested in alternatives to a traditional lawn, no problem! We've got you covered there, too, with topics such as, groundcover plants, rock gardens, flower beds, and vegetable gardens. A lawn shouldn't be your only option if it doesn't make sense for your lifestyle or space.

And, what if your current lawn is a hot mess? Not to worry, there's a whole chapter dedicated to renovating and repairing a lawn that is out of hand. It's never too late to bring that lawn back to life!

Further on, we'll look at how to deal with just about every lawn care nightmare out there: weeds, pests, diseases, moss, drainage issues, you name it. I'll help you identify any problems and offer organic, sustainable solutions. That's right, I'll offer green lawn practices that are good for the planet, too.

If you're interested in starting a lawn care business, you're in the right place. We've got information on developing your business plan, estimating jobs, marketing your services, and more. Turn your passion into profit while building your dream career.

By the end of this book, you'll be a total lawn care pro! You'll understand exactly how to grow and maintain a thriving lawn. I'll impart all the knowledge and skills I've learned over the years so you can have your greenest, healthiest lawn ever. Sound like fun? Then, let's get growing! The ultimate lawn awaits.

Chapter 1
Understanding Your Lawn

1.1 Different Grass Types

When creating a beautiful, healthy lawn, selecting the right type of grass for your climate and needs is one of the most important decisions. Different grass varieties have adapted to thrive in certain environmental conditions, so choosing well-suited varieties will reward you with an enviable lawn. Take time to understand the characteristics of each grass type and which fits best for your region and lawn goals.

The major categories of grasses used in residential lawns include cool-season grasses that flourish in northern states and warm-season grasses better suited to southern regions. Cool-season grasses tolerate cold winters and grow best in spring and fall when temperatures are cooler—types like fescue, bluegrass, and ryegrass fall in this group. Warm-season grasses embrace hot summers, going dormant in winter and then greening up as temperatures rise. Bermuda grass, zoysia, St. Augustine, and buffalograss are common warm-season varieties.

When selecting grass seed or sod, avoid the mistake of basing choices simply on the lush appearance you've seen in other lawns. That attractive grass may fail miserably in your own yard if your conditions don't match. Seek out grasses tested by universities to thrive in climates and soils similar to yours. State extension offices are great resources for guidance on varieties proven in local conditions.

Beyond climate, factor in other needs like shade or sun tolerance, durability, and usage. For example, northern lawns under tree canopies or with poor sunlight often benefit from shade-loving fescues. High-traffic areas and play spaces may call for tougher ryegrasses or zoysias. Maintenance preferences are also key - Kentucky bluegrass requires significant care, while Bermudas are more resilient.

Monoculture lawns of just one grass type were once common, but today's best practices promote biodiverse mixes tailored to microclimates within your yard. Blending compatible grasses creates layered canopies that inhibit weeds and sustain health even if one component is compromised. For example, mixing several top-rated regional varieties of fescue creates biodiversity. Just be sure all components share preferences for sun, soil, traffic, and maintenance.

When establishing a new lawn, select quality seed blends or sod with verified contents, preferable to generic seed. Beyond species, cultivar matters - new, improved varieties offer better disease resistance, color, drought tolerance, and other traits. Pay a little extra for premium, certified seed and sod, as the years of improved performance will prove the value.

Regardless of which grass types you select, always prepare the soil well with proper grading, drainage, and amendments to enable the grasses to thrive. Maintain optimal mowing, watering, fertilizing, and pest control practices consistently over time. When you match the right grasses to your climate and care for them properly, you will be rewarded with a lush, vigorous lawn for years to come. Now let's explore some of the most common cool-season and warm-season grass types to understand their particular characteristics and ideal uses:

Tall fescue is a cool-season bunch grass with deep roots that make it quite drought-tolerant. It has a medium green color and requires moderate maintenance. Tall fescue handles cold winters well and is commonly used across northern transition zones. Numerous improved cultivars exist, including Falcon IV, Firecracker LS, and Wolfpack.

Perennial ryegrass is established quickly for fast germination when seeding. It has very fine blades and a dark green hue but requires significant maintenance including, frequent watering. Ryegrass tolerates moderate traffic and transitions well into cool northern lawns when overseeded. Some newer hybrids like Reynolds provide durable wear tolerance.

Kentucky bluegrass is prized for its lush, rich blue-green beauty but demands extensive care. It needs ample moisture and frequent mowing and fertilization to look its best, but it doesn't tolerate drought or traffic well. Bluegrass excels when given ideal conditions. Improved varieties like Diva, Moonshadow, and Prosperity have better disease resistance.

Bermudagrass is a hardy, drought-resistant warm-season grass with good traffic capacity. It thrives in hot southern climates, going brown and dormant in winter, then bouncing back. Bermuda tolerates salt and resists insects but develops thatch quickly if overfertilized and needs dethatching. Yukon, Celebration, Tifway 419, and TifTuf are top bermudas.

Zoysia is another warm-season favorite due to its fine texture and tolerance of heat, cold, and drought. Dense zoysia crowds out weeds effectively once established but demands full sun and can be slow-growing. Emerald, Zeon, L1F, and Geo are exceptional zoysia cultivars. Zoysia makes a supreme grass for southern lawns and golf courses.

St. Augustine thrives in tropical climates and warmer coastal regions. It tolerates salt, resists chinch bugs, and fills in completely with stolons. St. Augustine needs good drainage, ample moisture, and pruning in the shade, or it thins out. Floratam, Bitterblue, Palmetto, and Sapphire are improved St. Augustine varieties.

Whichever grass you choose, always purchase top-rated seed guaranteed to be pure, weed-free, and with excellent germination rates. For sod, verify the grass species, cultivar, and avoid yellowing. While the best seed or sod may cost slightly more upfront, the long-term benefits make it worth investing in an exceptional lawn. With so many outstanding grass options now available, you can select an ideal blend to craft a stunning lawn tailored to your home.

1.2 Climate Considerations

The climate in your region plays a huge role in determining which grass varieties will thrive on your lawn. Factors like seasonal temperatures, humidity, rainfall, wind, and more impact growth. Selecting grasses genetically adapted to your local environment leads to healthier, easier-to-maintain lawns.

Start by understanding your area's USDA Hardiness Zone based on average annual minimum temperatures. Zones range from 1a in far northern areas to 13b in Hawaii and Puerto Rico. Cool-season grasses like fescues prefer zones 2-, while warm-season options like Bermuda excel in zones 7-10. Transition zone lawns can often support both types. This gives a baseline for grass selection.

Beyond zones, look at specific temperature and moisture trends year-round in making choices. For example, northern Kentucky bluegrass lawns can require irrigation in hot, dry summers, while coastal California climates are more temperate and conducive to low-water use tall fescues. Study regional university turf trials to see real-world performance in conditions mirroring your own.

The amount and distribution of annual precipitation also guide grass selection for a location. Frequent rainfall encourages lush turfgrasses like ryegrass, which would require irrigation in drier climates. But periods of drought favor durable, deep-rooted varieties better equipped to weather temporary dry spells without support. Whenever possible, choose native grasses already acclimated to natural rainfall in a region.

Humidity levels tie closely to precipitation and temperatures in indicating which grasses will thrive. Warm, humid climates allow St. Augustine and zoysia to flourish, while cool, arid regions are better suited to fescues and ryegrasses. New cultivars bred specifically for humidity tolerance can expand options in muggy areas once unfavorable.

Wind exposure is another important factor, especially in coastal and plains areas. Grasses that spread by above-ground stolons like Bermuda can fare better in windy locales than bunch grasses like fescue with less stolon development. Using protective wind barriers when first establishing lawns can aid success.

While summer conditions dominate grass growth, cold winter temperatures influence survivorship especially for warm-season varieties like zoysia and Bermuda. Evaluate each grass type's frost tolerance and winter hardiness specifically for your area.

When selecting the ideal grass types, dissect the unique climate profile for your location across seasonal variations, temperature, rainfall, humidity, prevailing winds, and winter extremes. This climate-matching process will ensure you choose lawn grasses genetically equipped to flourish. Beyond general regional climate, it's also important to understand the microclimates within your individual yard. Areas along tree lines, in rain shadows, on slopes, near water features, or with other unique characteristics can create localized conditions that diverge from the norm. Observe these carefully and select grass varieties accordingly.

For example, a lawn with a mix of full sun and dense shade microclimates calls for using shade-tolerant grass like fine fescue in shaded zones, while sun-loving Bermuda could still thrive in unobstructed areas. Or swales and drainage ditches may stay too wet for standard grasses, benefiting from flood-tolerant varieties like seashore paspalum. Tailor grass species around diverse microconditions.

If your local climate presents challenges like extreme aridity, high salinity, or periods of heavy shade, don't despair. Thanks to intensive grass breeding programs, you can now find grasses even adapted to difficult settings once considered inhospitable to lush lawns. For instance, new salt-tolerant Bermuda grasses like Salam and U-3 let coastal gardeners enjoy greener lawns despite saline soils.

Transition zone climates with hot summers and freezing winters can successfully mix cool-season and warm-season grasses. Winter overseeding with perennial ryegrass protects dormant Bermuda. Irrigated lawns in arid regions remain lush by selecting drought-resistant fescues. Seek guidance from local experts on combining grasses for challenging areas.

While matching grass species to current conditions is ideal, consider any long-term climate shift projections for your region. Gradual trends like increased aridity in Southwestern states or warmer winters in northern areas may warrant adjusting selections to ensure future lawn health. Seek grasses with resilience to withstand forecasted changes.

No matter what climate-related challenges your location presents, rest assured there are grass species and specialized varieties being bred to thrive there. Connect with regional universities, extension agents, local nurseries, and online forums to tap into climate-matching knowledge for your specific area. With thoughtful grass selection tailored to your precise conditions, you can enjoy lush, vibrant lawns even in demanding environments.

1.3 Soil Needs

The foundation of a thriving lawn begins below the surface with healthy soil. Different grass species thrive in specific soil conditions, so testing accordingly and amending your soil is key. Evaluating characteristics like soil texture, structure, pH, and nutrients allows you to create an optimal environment tailored to your chosen grass.

Soil texture refers to the relative proportions of sand, silt, and clay particles. Sandy soils drain quickly but lack water and nutrient retention, while heavy clay soils resist drainage and dry out slowly. Loams with a blend of particle sizes offer an ideal balance. Soil texture influences multiple lawn care practices, such as irrigation needs, fertilization frequency, and aeration requirements.

Simple jar tests provide a general assessment to determine your predominant soil type. Mix a soil sample in water and shake, allowing particles to settle based on size. Sand rapidly drops to the bottom, silt forms a middle layer, and clay stays suspended. Compare the ratios to estimate your texture. More complex lab particle size analyses can provide precise percentages.

In addition to texture, a soil's structure affects lawn health. Granular, crumbly soils with good aggregation allow air and water movement while heavily compacted layers resist penetration. Regular aeration maintains the structure and prevents compaction. Evaluate a fresh soil sample - clumpy and loose indicates better structure than solid, dense soil. Healthy grass balances soil texture and structure.

Next, testing the pH level is crucial since grasses thrive within acidic to alkaline ranges. Most perform best around neutral 6.5-7 pH. Kits measure pH in water or buffer solutions. Acidic soils can be treated with lime applications, while sulfurr lowers alkalinity if needed. Match target pH to your grass species' preferences.

Complete nutrient testing identifies any deficiencies limiting growth. Major macronutrients like nitrogen, phosphorous, and potassium are commonly supplemented with micronutrients. Again, grass species vary in optimal nutritional profiles and concentrations. Custom fertilizer blends and organic amendments can restore proportions suitable for your grass.

Finally, evaluating soil salinity, cation exchange capacity, and organic matter provides additional useful indicators to create the ideal soil environment. Take time to thoroughly analyze each characteristic and adjust accordingly through grading, pH adjustment, fertilization, and amendment applications. Proper soil preparation allows grasses to flourish fully. When installing a new lawn, soil preparation provides a golden opportunity to modify and enhance your native soils as needed. Planning construction projects around the ideal lawn timeline allows grading, excavation, amendment addition, and development of the perfect mature soil.

For example, during initial site grading, blend in sandy loam topsoil to improve water drainage and nutrient-holding capacity in dense clay soils. Or add organic compost, manure, peat, or other amendments to boost soil structure and microbial activity in compacted soils. Investing time and resources to optimize soil conditions before seeding or laying sod pays off for years.

Alternatively, you can incrementally improve the soil in an existing lawn over time. Regular core aeration helps alleviate compaction and increase air and water movement. Topdressings with quality compost or topsoil add organic matter to enrich the upper profile. Adjusting pH and targeting fertilizer applications address nutrition needs. Overseeding fills in thin areas. While slower, steady enhancements make a difference.

Complete renovations may be justified for lawns with severely compromised soil to rehabilitate the growing envirnoment. This involves stripping away old sod, aerating subsoils, grading, and blending amendments to create an ideal new medium. Such measures can redeem even poor soils into excellent grass growth conditions if planned well.

When renovating, incorporating dynamic features like subsurface drainage tiles, catch basins, or retention areas allows for optimally managing moisture levels. Installing in-ground irrigation systems permits applying controlled amounts of water exactly when needed. Keep soil conditioning in mind if making landscape changes.

The soil supporting your lawn should be viewed as a constantly evolving ecosystem. Regular care sustains soil biodiversity, structure, and nutrient recycling to benefit your grass. Simple practices like mulching clippings, overseeding, fertilizing, and amending stimulate biological activity and tilth. Healthy soils mean healthy grass.

Commit to caring for the soils supporting your lawn as thoughtfully as the grass plants themselves. While soil needs vary by grass species, tailoring your soil's physical and chemical makeup to match selected grasses will provide an ideal foundation for lush, vigorous turfgrass. Proper soils transform a space from mere dirt into a vibrant plant ecosystem.

1.4 Sunlight Requirements

The amount of direct sunlight reaching your lawn area significantly affects the grass species able to thrive there. Most lawn grasses require at least 6 hours of direct sun daily for vigorous growth and to deter weed invasions into thinner turf. Evaluating sunlight patterns guides appropriate grass selection and care.

Full sun lawns receive the highest light levels - at least 8-10 hours of direct sun exposure over more than 90% of the yard. These conditions allow the widest range of grass types to succeed, including sun-loving warm-season grasses like bermudagrass. Choose any grass suited to your climate and maintenance preferences for full sun settings.

Partial sun lawns see 4-6 hours of unfiltered sun over at least half the yard. Transition zone lawns often fall into this range. Cool-season grasses like fescues and ryegrasses grow well here, as do some warmer-season grasses. Avoid types needing full sun exposure.

Shaded lawns receive 2 hours or less of direct sun over most of the area. Dense tree canopies create dry shade, minimizing grass growth. Fine fescues offer the best shade tolerance, along with some improved ryegrass and zoysia cultivars. Cool-season grasses fare better than warm-season types in shade.

When assessing sunlight, note the aspect or cardinal direction the lawn faces. South or wes- facing locations receive much more sunlight intensity than north or east orientations because of the sun's arc. Account for these differences when planning. Also, observe seasonal variations based on sun angle and tree leaf cycles.

Use the shadow test to estimate sunlight levels by standing in the center of your lawn area and observing the shadow you cast at noon. A very short or no shadow indicates full sun. Moderate-length shadows suggest partial sun. Full shade exists if your shadow completely covers the lawn space.

You can also use smartphone apps to track sunlight duration and hours in specific lawn zones. Compare findings to your grass species' recommended minimum hours. Supplement with shade cloth or selective pruning if light levels are insufficient for the desired grass.

When laying new sod or seed, existing sunlight levels dictate grass selection. You may need to transition to shade-tolerant grasses over time by overseeding for established lawns with changing light die to mature trees. Proper sunlight drives photosynthesis and growth, so choose and maintain grasses matched to light levels. In addition to daily sunlight levels, seasonal light variation is an important consideration. Winter shadows cast by trees and buildings are much longer than summer shadows. Evergreen trees block more sunlight in fall and winter when deciduous trees are bare.

Account for these seasonal light changes when selecting grass varieties. For example, a lawn may receive sufficient sun in summer for Bermuda grass but thin out in winter shade. Adding ryegrass as an overseeded winter companion grass compensates for reduced light.

Morning and afternoon sun differs too - morning light is weaker while afternoon has greater intensity. If the lawn slopes, one aspect may be brighter than another. Ideally, choose grasses suited to the lowest light levels for sustainability.

If an existing lawn receives too little light for the current grass type, you can take measures to increase sunlight. Selective tree pruning to open the canopy helps significantly. For small yards, removing problematic trees altogether may be an option. Relocating shrubs or other landscaping can also allow more light to reach the lawn.

When working around mature trees, avoid damage to the tree's health when pruning. Never remove more than 25% of theliving tree canopy within a single season. Cutting main branches should be done carefully to avoid permanent injury. Engage a certified arborist for major tree work.

For adjacent properties where off-site trees create shade issues, discuss options for selective pruning with your neighbor. Offer to split the cost of professional pruning for mutual benefit. Use fencing, vines, or decorative screens to mask overly shaded areas.

Supplementing with artificial lighting is generally not practical for residential lawns. But lighting used for nighttime enjoyment can contribute some photosynthetic benefit. Position walkway or landscape lights strategically to cast additional illumination on the lawn.

If poor sunlight cannot be sufficiently improved through pruning or other measures, transition to shade-tolerant grasses or alternative shade landscaping. Interplanting ornamentals and groundcovers becomes an option in dense shade situations with minimal direct sun.

While most lawns require good sun, there are solutions for making even shady sites lush and enjoyable. Adjust expectations and choose shade-appropriate plants. With care, even challenging low-light lawns can be transformed into beautiful and functional spaces.

1.5 Lawn Size and Shape

When planning a new lawn or renovating an existing one, evaluating the overall size and shape of the yard area is an important early step. This helps determine everything from grass species and irrigation design to mowing equipment needs and maintenance workload. Carefully considering dimensions and geometry helps create a vibrant lawn scaled appropriately.

Measure the total square footage of your potential lawn space. Irregularly shaped yards may need sectioning into rectangles or triangles to estimate accurately. This establishes the total grass area and gives perspective on the extent of upkeep required. Even a modest-appearing lawn can exceed 10,000 sq ft, requiring significant mowing, watering, and care.

Also, measure any unusable areas like slopes greater than 3:1 that cannot safely be mowed or accessed. Beds around trees, gardens, and hardscapes should be excluded from the lawn zone. Subtract these spaces when calculating your turfgrass footprint.

Next, assess the proportions and geometry of the lawn area. Is it a large contiguous expanse or fragmented into multiple small sections? What is the length-to-width ratio? How curved or irregular is the perimeter? All these traits inform suitable grass species and equipment.

For example, a long, narrow lawn presents challenges for turning mowing equipment. Tighter spaces favor compact models with greater maneuverability. Broad open lawns can accommodate wider cutting swaths and riding mowers. Fragmented lawn sections divided by beds or hardscapes may require multiple mower passes from different angles.

Also, consider the practicality of access points to the lawn. Can equipment and materials be easily transported in and around the full area? Steep slopes or stairs may limit specific renovation machinery. Insufficient access can hinder maintenance significantly. If access is constrained, reduce lawn sizes or create permeable hardscape paths.

Take note of any obstructions like trees, signs, and play equipment within the lawn area. Allow adequate clearance for safe mowing and trimming around these features. If obstacles are excessive or clustered, excluding zones from the main lawn may be wise.

The shape and proportions of your lawn should suit the desired functionality, be realistically maintainable given space constraints, and provide an aesthetic complement to the overall landscape. Good planning and care can make even unusually shaped and sized yards into beautiful healthy lawns. For existing lawns, reevaluate the established dimensions and geometry to identify any changes needed. Lawns often shrink over time from encroachments like expanding landscape beds, patios, and play areas. Reclaiming lost turf areas is easier during renovations.

Also, look for opportunities to remove rarely used or hard-to-mow sections from the main lawn. For example, isolating space-consuming perimeter strips along fences often improves mowing ease and allows edging beds. Repurposing awkward lawn pans into mulch beds also reduces maintenance.

If the current lawn area exceeds your needs or maintenance abilities, reducing its footprint may be wise. Prioritize the most visible or functional areas as primary lawn space, converting excess to alternative groundcovers or hardscapes. Less trafficked zones around the home's perimeter also make ideal sites to revert to low-care landscaping.

Properly delineating and edging all lawn boundaries maximizes usable area and simplifies mowing. Installing borders like stone edges, timbers, or metal strips maintains a clear divide between turfgrass and adjacent beds or materials. This avoids time-consuming hand trimming.

If applicable, consider lawn geometry with the distance limitations of your current irrigation system. Expand coverage for any areas chronically drying out due to insufficient water delivery. Evaluate if lawn proportions align well with sprinkler reach or if modifications would improve irrigation efficiency.

As with any landscape element, consider how the lawn's size, shape, and siting impact aesthetics and views. Use gradual curves and creative contours to lend visual interest. Make sure the lawn proportions and layout complement the home's architecture and other hardscapes.

Whether starting from scratch or modifying existing turf areas, take time to thoughtfully envision the ideal lawn footprint specific to your property. Map it out, accounting for functional needs, easy maintenance, irrigation practicality, and attractive geometry. Your lawn's dimensions and configuration fundamentally influence its ongoing care.

1.6 Existing Landscape

The characteristics of landscapes surrounding a lawn significantly influence the lawn's health and maintenance. Evaluating existing trees, gardens, hardscapes, and topography provides key insights for planning a new or renovated lawn area. Thoughtfully integrating turf grass with other features creates a cohesive, sustainable landscape.

Survey mature trees on the property and within 50 feet of lawn borders. Root zones, rain interception, leaf litter, and shade patterns from trees impact lawn viability in areas adjacent to or beneath trees. Provide sufficient clearance between trees and lawn edges to allow mowing and prevent root competition.

Also, assess the shade and leaf debris produced by trees overhanging the planned lawn. Excess shade limits grass growth—plan for fall leaf litter removal in lawn areas near deciduous trees. Evergreen boughs also shed needles on the lawn. Avoid turfgrass directly beneath dense trees where performance will suffer.

Take note of existing gardens and beds around or within the potential lawn space. Avoid complex geometry and fragmentation where beds bisect turf areas. This complicates mowing. Simplify any adjacent bed lines abutting lawn sections for easier edging and trimming.

Review current hardscapes like patios, walkways, and driveways bordering the lawn. Look for opportunities to extend hardscapes along areas challenging to mow, such as narrow side strips. Any turf abutting hard edges requires trimming or edging. Reduce these demanding transitional zones.

Examine the overall topography and any slopes encompassing or within the planned lawn. Steep slopes exceeding 3:1 present safety hazards for mowing and offer poor growing conditions. Consider alternative groundcovers on inclines over 10 degrees. Integrate terracing if retaining any steep sections.

Observe water drainage across the site. Avoid low wet spots with poor drainage. Design any necessary earthworks and subsurface drainage early before establishing lawn areas. Install catch basins, dry riverbeds, rain gardens, or retention swales to manage runoff responsibly.

The goal is to smoothly integrate a new or renovated lawn within the surrounding landscape. Avoid fragmented, irregularly shaped turf areas challenging to mow and edge. Enhance topography to direct drainage responsibly. Blend lawn spaces cohesively with existing trees, beds, and hardscapes. For existing lawns, inspect areas bordering other landscapes closely to identify issues. Turf areas encroached by tree roots or expanding beds become difficult to maintain over time. Redefine edges and reclaim lawn space during renovations where feasible.

Extend beds outward if the current lawn-bed interface is irregular or too narrow to mow cleanly. For example, converting a 12-inch perimeter lawn strip to shrub borders or mulch beds simplifies maintenance. Evaluate eliminating any isolated islands of remaining turf.

However, balance reclaimed lawn area against total mowing and watering reductions. Converting 500 square feet of lawn edge to beds makes little impact on a 10,000 square-foot lawn. Focus conversions on excess lawn sections providing minimal function or aesthetic value.

Use edging tools to reestablish clean dividers and straight lines where beds meet lawns. Install plastic, metal, or stone borders to maintain separation long-term. This avoids time-consuming string trimming needed when bed edges fade. Crisp borders enhance visual appeal.

Where existing trees within or around lawns will remain, take proactive steps to reduce negative impacts on turf health. Vertical mulching trenches radiating outward from the trunk decompact soil and encourage roots to grow downward rather than horizontally.

Pruning the lower limbs of mature trees opens the canopy for more light penetration. Consult a certified arborist to perform this properly without harming the tree. Regularly rake fallen leaves in autumn to prevent smothering grass.

For chronic lawn wet spots due to runoff or poor drainage, consider French drains, catch basins with sump pumps, or regraded swales to divert water. Target the source of moisture rather than trying to sustain turfgrass in soggy soil.

Whether renovating an existing landscape or planning new construction, keep the interplay between lawn space and other elements in mind from the outset. This holistic view allows the creation of integrated, complementary designs that enhance the property visually and functionally.

25

Chapter 2
Lawn Care 101

2.1 Mowing Tips

Proper mowing practices are essential for maintaining a healthy, attractive lawn. Mowing accomplishes several important functions - controlling excessive top growth, scalping weed tops to reduce seeding, and forceing dense turf growth that chokes out weeds. However, improper mowing can damage grass plants, introduce disease, and degrade the lawn over time.

Follow the 1/3 rule - never cut more than 1/3 of the grass blade height at any mowing. For cool-season grasses like fescue, aim for a final height of around 3 inches after mowing. Warm-season grasses can be mowed shorter to 1-2 inches if desired. Taking off no more than 1/3 avoids scalping and shocking the plants.

Mow frequently enough so that no more than 1/3 of the blade length needs removing at each pass. For fast-growing grasses, this may mean mowing every 4-5 days at peak growth. Reduce frequency as growth naturally slows. At least weekly mowing is recommended for most lawns during the growing season.

Keep mower blades extremely sharp to ensure clean cuts rather than shredding or tearing blades. Sharpen blades after every 8-10 hours of use. Dull or damaged blades give grass tips a brown, shaggy appearance. Clean-cutting is healthier for the plants.

Vary mowing patterns between sessions - mow north-south one time, then east-west for the next session. This prevents rutting, graining, and soil compaction from wheels repeatedly following the same paths. Alternate directions yield a more even cut and prevent lawn grooves.

Mow when the grass is cool and dry, typically early morning or evening, to avoid heat stress. Avoid mowing wet grass, which clumps and leads to an uneven cut. Never remove more than 1/3 blade length when mowing wet or drought-stressed grass.

Set mower deck height for the species and conditions. Raise for stressed or shaded lawns to compensate for slower growth. Keep tne deck clear of clippings that block airflow - clean after each use. Proper mowing height and blade maintenance let your mower perform its best. Start on the outside border and work inward in concentric rows when mowing.. This contains clippings within the lawn area rather than discharging them onto beds or driveways around the perimeter. For large open areas, mow back and forth between two edges.

Overlap mowing swaths slightly for complete coverage without any missed strips. For lawns with a lot of obstacles or contour changes, manually outline the perimeter first, then work inward sections to avoid leaving uncut areas. Take time for precision trimming around trees, gardens, and other obstructions.

Let turfgrass fully dry after heavy rain before mowing again. Wet grass clumps on the deck and the height beneath the wheels damages tender blades. Well drained lawns may dry adequately the next day. Poorly drained lawns likely need an extra few days before mowing.

Adjust mowing pace for conditions - mow more slowly in thick, damp grass. Faster speeds work for dry turf with good density. Vary speed when turning and overlapping passes to avoid skipping spots or rutting around the perimeter. Take time to mow carefully.

For weed control, cut tall weeds and seed heads Separately before mowing the main lawn, collecting rather than mulching this initial trimming. Target weedy areas again on the final lawn pass. Weed tops left on the lawn can still mature seeds after mowing.

Clean the underside of the mowing deck thoroughly after each use to remove all grass clippings, debris, and standing moisture. Built-up clippings impact cutting efficiency and contribute to blade rusting. Regular under-deck cleaning is essential.

Proper mowing technique provides the well-kept carpeted appearance we desire from quality turfgrass. Following sound mowing practices strengthens grass plants, discourages weeds, and improves lawn aesthetics. Make mowing a priority throughout the growing season.

2.2 Watering Guidelines

Watering appropriately fosters deep, resilient grass roots while avoiding fungal diseases. Proper irrigation also conserves water, which is increasingly precious in many regions. Match watering practices to your specific lawn's needs and monitor effects. Overwatering is just as detrimental as underwatering.

Water early in the morning, between 4-10 a.m., when evaporation rates are lowest. Avoid midday watering, which wastes much water to evaporation. Evening watering leaves grass damp overnight, promoting fungal issues. Morning is ideal for a good soaking.

Apply water infrequently but deeply, moistening the entire root zone depth each time. Shallow daily sprinkling trains roots to stay near the surface, making grass vulnerable to drying out. Prioritize deep weekly or twice-weekly soaking while avoiding runoff.

Adjust run times and frequency based on weather conditions, avoiding preset rigid schedules. More water is needed during hot, dry periods. Reduce during rainy or cool stretches. Inspect soil moisture visually or with a probe to judge actual water needs.

Allow the soil surface to partially dry out between watering. Proper drying strengthens roots, while anaerobic, soggy soil weakens them. The drying period depends on soil type - sandy soils drain quickly while clay stays moist longer before the next required watering.

Calibrate sprinklers to apply 1-1.5 inches per hour maximum to avoid a wasteful runoff. Position sprinklers to achieve head-to-head coverage without dry spots. Split the total run times into shorter cycles allowing soak in between.

Let grass grow longer in hot months to provide insulating shade for soil and reduce water demand. Taller grass blades lose less moisture to evaporation and transpire less than closely mown turfgrass.

Use tuna cans or other straight-sided containers placed in sprinkler zones to gauge application rates. Adjust run times and head placement as needed until each zone applies water evenly at desired rates. During drought or mandatory water restrictions, allow the lawn to discolor and enter summer dormancy if needed. The grass crowns will survive extended dormancy and green up upon rewatering. Prioritize tree and shrub health over perfect summer turf color.

Consider installing an automatic moisture sensor controller to precisely irrigate based on actual soil dryness. These conserve water compared to timers and adjust for weather variation. More affordable options are rain sensors that delay watering cycles after rainfall.

Improve irrigation efficiency with equipment upgrades like rotating sprinkler nozzles to apply water more uniformly. Identify and adjust areas with overspray to avoid wasting water like nearby pavement. Drip irrigation works well for trees, beds and sloped zones.

Hand watering with hoses allows precise spot treatment of dry or damaged areas as needed instead of soaking the entire lawn. Be sure to distribute the water thoroughly. Moving hoses frequently prevents puddling.

Evaluate lawn water distribution by observing color differences. Dark green areas signal excess water, which promotes shallow roots and fungal issues. Brown patches obviously need more moisture. A uniform color indicates balanced water.

Inspect sprinklers seasonally for clogged or broken nozzles causing uneven coverage. Straighten tilted heads digging into the turf. Replace worn nozzle screens and gaskets to maintain proper spray patterns, preventing dry spots.

For automatic systems, check the control box power supply, wiring condition, solenoid valve function, and backflow device annually before peak season. Make repairs so the system operates reliably when needed.

Proper irrigation applied at the right intervals is crucial to growing a resilient, healthy lawn. Monitor grass condition and soil moisture levels to inform watering schedules. Improve equipment and practices over time for peak efficiency.

2.3 Fertilizing Schedules

Applying the right fertilizers at optimal times nourishes grass plants, fuels growth, and crowds out weeds. However, improper fertilization harms the lawn and wastes money. Wise use of quality fertilizers tailored to your grass type and season delivers a vibrant, healthy lawn.

Always select a balanced fertilizer with a mix of fast and slow-release nitrogen, phosphate for root growth, and potassium for wear resistance and drought tolerance. Avoid overapplying high nitrogen products, which damage soil ecology.

Read labels closely - lawn fertilizer will list a three-number N-P-K ratio indicating percentages of nitrogen, phosphorous and potassium as nutrients. Aim for moderate ratios around 20-5-15 for typical conditions.

Time fertilizer applications appropriately for your particular grass species and climate. Warm-season grasses thrive with spring and summer feeding. Cool-season grasses prosper with fallfeedings—match fertilizer timing to grass growth cycles.

Apply at manufacturer-recommended rates - more is not better. Excessive fertilizer harms grass, soils, and waterways. Target a maximum of 2-4 pounds of nitrogen per year per 1000 sq ft as. Carefully calibrate your spreader.

Slow-release organic fertilizers are safest for overall soil and grass health, avoiding synthetic quick-release salts. Quality compost, meal, and pellet blends work well. Top-dress lawns annually with 1/4 inch of compost.

Water in soluble fertilizers like urea immediately after spreading to avoid the burning potential on leaf blades from fertilizer salts. Granular fertilizers do not require fast watering but still need rainfall or irrigation soon to dissolve and soak into the soil.

Mow lawn first, then fertilize optimally 1-2 days later, allowing grass plants to rebound from any mowing stress before feeding. Never fertilize right before or after major lawn stress like weed control or aeration. Observe lawn response in the weeks following fertilization to gauge effectiveness. Look for a moderate flush of new growth, greener color, and increased density. If excessive growth results, reduce application rates next round.

Alternate soluble quick-release fertilizers with slower organic options during the growing season. The quick green-up helps complement the soil-building benefits and safer application of organics.

Adjust plans if soil tests reveal any significant nutritional deficiencies or excesses. Target fertilizers and amendments to restore proper balances rather than applying them broadly. Review soil tests every 2-3 years to guide adjustments.

When laying new sod or seed, delay initial fertilizer application until the grass has rooted and established. New plantings often come pre-fertilized from the source. Wait until initial mowing to begin light feeding.

As the lawn grows denser later in the season, increase mowing height before fertilizing. This avoids excessive top growth resulting from the feeding. Let grass grow taller before applying late-season fertilizer.

Scatter the fertilizer by spreading it evenly to cover the entire lawn without gaps or overlaps, leading to an inconsistent application. Calibrate the spreader settings and walk at a steady pace in a criss-cross pattern for full, even coverage.

Sweep any fertilizer scattering onto paved surfaces back into the turf to avoid washing into storm drains. Never apply before heavy rains that would similarly wash nutrients away rather than soaking them in the soil.

Proper fertilization rewards you with a vibrant green lawn that maintains health and fights off weeds. But more is not better - carefully follow rates and timing for your specific grass type. Consistent light feeding prevents overdose issues.

2.4 Aerating Benefits

Core aeration is vital for relieving soil compaction and improving lawn health. Over time, foot traffic, mowing, and inadequate aeration cause hard, impenetrable soils, preventing air, water, and nutrients from reaching grass roots. Aerating remedies this through hollow tine extraction. The aeration process removes small plugs of soil 3-4 inches deep across the lawn, leaving holes to alleviate compaction. Core spacing is typically 2-3 inches with numerous passes to thoroughly aerate, and the holes are not backfilled.

There are many benefits to lawn aeration.It relieves soil compaction, allowing better air, water, and nutrient infiltration into root zones. It reduces water runoff and puddling by improving drainage. Aeration enables stronger, deeper grass roots to expand into the loosened soil. The holes provide entry points to introduce topdressing compounds like organic matter, sand, or gypsum to improve overall soil quality. Aeration also minimizes thatch buildup by increasing microbial activity in the soil to break down excess organic material. Finally, it reduces mechanical impedance for smoother mowing over uneven terrain.

The best times to aerate are spring and fall when grass is actively growing and can quickly recover from the disruption of the process. The soil cores decay over 2-3 weeks, so you want to aerate when daytime air temperatures support strong root growth. Avoid summer heat or freezing winter conditions. Core aeration only removes a small percentage of soil per pass, so that it can be performed routinely. Applying annually in the fall is ideal for most lawns, but higher-traffic areas may benefit from biannual or quarterly sessions. Be sure to give the lawn adequate time to rebound between aeration sessions.

Proper core depth is essential - extraction must reach below any compacted layer, usually 3-4 inches for home lawns, unless a hardpan exists deeper. Dethatching to remove any matted layers should be performed before aerating so the soil cores can be extracted from beneath the thatch. Use hollow tines 0.5-0.75 inches wide to remove maximum soil. The speed passing the aerator over the lawn is also key - work slowly enough to achieve completel soil plug extraction without excessively tearing turf. Let the tines do the work without forcing them. Some liquid coming to the surface is normal. Re-seed any damaged spots afterwards. When core aerating, make several perpendicular passes across the lawn to thoroughly penetrate from multiple directions. For cool-season grasses, aim to extract 15-20 cores per square foot each session. Warm-season grasses that spread via above-ground stolons recover quicker and can handle up to 40 plugs per square foot if needed. Visually inspect extraction density after passes and make additional runs over compacted areas.

Prior to aerating, mow the lawn shorter than usual to allow easy tine penetration without catching and tearing blades. Remove any debris like sticks which could clog or damage equipment. Ensure the soil is moist but not saturated to allow for clean plug extraction - water a day or two prior if the soil is bone dry. Work the topdressing into holes from a broadcast spreader between aeration passes.

For best results, core aerate in one direction, then make cross-direction passes. Vary the angle occasionally to reach areas side-by-side tines may miss. Make sure to overlap passes about one tine width to cover the entire lawn, avoiding any gaps. Take added passes around high-traffic zones and compacted edges. Shady areas and heavy clay soils likely need extra aeration attention as well.

If possible, time core acration just before applying fertilizer and overseeding. This allows nutrients and seed good soil contact. However, wait 2-4 weeks if also applying weed control around the same timeframe to reduce turfgrass stress. Top dress aeration holes with quality compost or a mix of compost and sand to smooth and fill holes, filtering in gradually over weeks.

Proper lawn aeration relieves compaction, encourages deep roots, enhances drainage, feeds the soil ecosystem, reduces thatch, and smooths an uneven surface. Make this often overlooked task a regular routine each year. Aerating improves overall lawn performance and health noticeably over time. Thatching before and topdressing afterward maximize benefits further.

For renovations on lawns with extreme compaction, consider more aggressive tine-free aeration methods like liquid core aeration or tractor-pulled slicing/plugging machines. But routine hollow tine extraction suffices for maintaining the most established lawns. Just be sure to aerate sufficiently based on square footage and inspect results. Proper aeration pays off with a vibrant, smooth lawn by renovating the soil structure.

2.5 Dethatching Essentials

Dethatching removes accumulated layers of dead grass stems and roots, called thatch, from the lawn surface. Excess thatch buildup causes numerous problems that dethatching alleviates. Like aerating, dethatching improves soil contact, growth, and appearance.

Thatch is a tightly intermingled organic layer above the soil surface composed of stems, roots, and trimmings that did not decompose. Some thatch is normal and beneficial, but excess beyond 1/2 inch blocks water, air, and nutrients from reaching the soil. Signs it's time to dethatch include: a thatch layer over 1/2 inch thick when measured, green color disappearing when thatch is peeled back, a bouncy feel when walking across the lawn, water pooling on the surface rather than soaking in, matted down grass that resists rebound when walked on, and moss invading in the mat layer.

Dethatching removes this excess layer and brings grass blades closer contact with soil. The main benefits include improved air exchange at the soil surface for better respiration, freer water penetration, and drainage to roots rather than runoff, open channels for better fertilizer contact and absorption into the soil, reduced moisture retention near crowns, prevention of fungal issues, and allows newly seeded grasses better contact for germination and establishment.

There are three main types of dethatching methods: Power raking uses a spinning bladed reel to physically tear into the thatch layer and rip it out. Tines may penetrate the soil slightly, but it is not true aeration. Best for serious thatch issues. Vertical mowing blades cut into the thatch and turf while leaving the soil intact. It stimulates growth but is less aggressive. Scarifying has fixed blades that scrape just below the surface, removing debris.

The amount of thatch removed depends on blade setting depth, number of passes made, and raking direction. First, make perpendicular passes to cover the whole area, then go over once or twice diagonally. Walk speed matters - working slowly enables the machine to remove material effectively with less turf damage. Overlap passes slightly for full coverage.

For cool-season grasses, aim to dethatch in early fall so turf can recover before winter dormancy. Warm-season grasses should be dethatched in early summer when actively growing. Avoid dethatching in excess heat or cold. Also, dethatching before core aeration allows tines better penetration.

After dethatching, rake or blow away debris, compost small amounts or collect with a mower bag attachment. Excessive thatch may require removal over several sessions to prevent turf shock. Reseed any damaged or bare areas. Topdress lightly with quality compost to fill uneven spots. While power raking is an aggressive option well-suited to removing heavy thatch accumulation, gentler methods like vertical mowing and scarifying blades often suffice for routine lawn maintenance with moderate thatch issues. The spinning vertical mower blades cut into the turf and thatch without disturbing the soil. This stimulates the grass to grow while removing debris.Vertical mowing or scarifying for routine dethatching is less stressful on the turf than power raking. For routine dethatching, vertical mowing or scarifying is less stressful on the turf compared to power raking.

The amount of thatch removed during the dethatching process depends on several factors - the depth setting of the blades, the number of passes made over the lawn, and the direction or pattern of passes. When operating the dethatcher, first make several perpendicular passes over the entire area to cover it completely. Then, go over the lawn once or twice at diagonal angles to the first direction. The number of total passes and overall raking time depends on the thickness of the debris layer. Work slowly and methodically enough for the machine to remove material effectively with each pass. Slightly overlapping the passes ensures full coverage without missing strips.

Proper timing of dethatching is important for lawn recovery. For cool-season grasses, aim to dethatch in early fall when cool-season lawns are still actively growing enough to recover before winter dormancy sets in. Warm-season grasses should be dethatched in early summer when night temperatures are reliably warm and in their active growing phase. Avoid dethatching during excess heat stress or frigid cold, as turfgrass plants will be vulnerable. It's also wise to dethatch before core aerating to allow the aeration tines better soil penetration.

After completing the dethatching, rake or blow away the pulled-up debris. Smaller amounts can be composted, but excess thatch may simply need removal if extensive. Severe thatch accumulation may require dethatching over several sessions to prevent excessive shock or damage to the turfgrass. Reseed any damaged or bare areas afterward to aid regrowth. Lightly topdress with quality compost to fill in uneven spots or holes. Proper follow-up care enables full lawn recovery after dethatching stress.

Routine dethatching and aeration maintain soil contact and health in established lawns. For neglected lawns with major thatch buildup, gradual removal over multiple seasons is preferable to sudden aggressive dethatching all at once. Adjusting mowing, watering, and fertilization practices can also reduce excessive thatch accumulation. But when needed, judicious dethatching provides strong benefits, improving drainage, appearance, and growth.

2.6 Overseeding Fundamentals

Overseeding replenishes thin or damaged areas of lawns by planting new grass seeds. It improves density, color, and durability. Routine overseeding enhances overall lawn quality over time. Reasons to overseed include:
Thinning or bare patches from pet urine, high traffic, etc.
Weed infestations where grass has died out.
Filling in new lawns that did not grow densely.
Improving lawn density and color.
Transitioning to new grass species or varieties.
Recovery from damage like disease, insects, or drought.

Proper timing is critical - overseed when temperatures remain above 50° F both day and night for several weeks after planting to enable germination and establishment. For cool-season grasses, overseed in early fall when temperatures cool, but ample growth weeks remain before winter dormancy. Late winter into early spring overseeding can also work depending on climate. Warm-season grasses should be overseeded in mid to late spring after soils have warmed but before peak summer heat arrives.

To prepare for overseeding:
Mow, dethatch, and aerate lawn ahead of time.
Remove existing weed growth through spraying or hand pulling.
Amend the soil in bare spots with quality compost tilled in.
Ensure good seed-to-soil contact by raking and leveling the area.
Select high-quality seeds well suited to your conditions.
Follow all label instructions carefully for application.

The best times to overseed align with periods right before the ideal growing seasons for the grass type. This gives new seedlings time to establish before being put to the test. Proper preparation also creates good conditions for germination and growth.

When selecting grass seed, choose a mix ideally containing several compatible species or varieties well-suited to your lawn's specific conditions. Use certified seed from reputable suppliers - higher quality seed has better germination rates for fuller results. For patching existing lawns, aim to match the original grass species unless transitioning varieties.

Application methods depend on the size of the area, seed type, and equipment available. Spread seed using a drop spreader for smaller spots, ensuring even coverage without gaps. For larger overseeding, use broadcast methods like a rotary spreader. Divide the area into sections and apply in two perpendicular passes for uniform distribution.

Rake the seed gently into the soil surface, then roll lightly or spread thin topdressing to maintain good contact. This gives some protection from birds and winds. Be careful raking not to disturb seeds in established lawn areas. Water newly seeded areas daily until germination, keeping the soil moist but not saturated. Once the new grass seedlings are established, usually 3-4 weeks after germination, overseeding care focuses on allowing the young grass to continue developing while avoiding competition from existing turf. Gradually reduce the watering frequency as the seedlings strengthen but supply ample moisture in early stages.

The first mowing after overseeding is delicate - set blades high to avoid harming tender new growth while cutting established lawn areas. Let new grass reach 3 inches before mowing gently. Follow normal mowing practices going forward, but inspect often for young seedling damage at first.

Application of starter fertilizer when seeding helps young roots establish. Follow up with lighter fertilization after 4-6 weeks for continued fill-in. Too much nitrogen initially can damage seedlings. Delay herbicide use until new grass matures. Spot-treat weeds manually in overseeded areas if needed.

Overseeded cool season grasses often enter winter dormancy sooner than mature surrounding turf. This causes temporary uneven color, but new growth will blend in come spring. Avoid high traffic in developing areas until the new grass matches the old for durability.

Transitional overseeding gradually shifts existing grass varieties by seeding increased percentages of the new desired blend each season. The improved type will dominate within 3-4 years, but a gradual transition avoids major lawn damage.

Alternate overseeding techniques like slit seeding may better disperse new seeds into established lawns. Slit seeders cut narrow grooves into the soil surface that seeds lodge within. This protects seeds and gives good soil contact.

Proper overseeding technique provides an affordable means of improving lawn density, color, quality, and functionality over time. Enhance thin or damaged areas in fall or spring based on grass type. With the right timing, seed selection, and follow-up care, overseeding thickens lawns effectively.

Chapter 3
Advanced Lawn Care

3.1 Soil Testing

While visual lawn assessment provides some insights, soil testing is the best way to understand your lawn's true nutritional status. Laboratory analysis of soil samples identifies pH, macronutrients, micronutrients, and other characteristics. Soil testing reveals potential deficiencies causing lawn problems, saves money on unneeded amendments, and provides science-based fertility recommendations. Testing every 2-3 years monitors soil changes over time. Proper sampling, accurate testing, and adhering to recommendations are key to success.

Take samples from across the lawn area using a soil probe or trowel from a consistent 3-6 inch depth, avoiding contaminated surface material. Extract 15-20 cores randomly dispersed across each 5,000 sq ft section to mix into a representative sample. Repeat for each unique section. Let samples air dry before placing them in sealable plastic bags labeled with the date and sample ID. Numerous public and private laboratories will analyze samples for around $25-50 per sample. Much lower-cost DIY test kits only scratch the surface, lacking accuracy.

Submit detailed background on your lawn species, environment, maintenance, and issues to inform recommendations. Complete basic analysis includes pH/acidity and lime requirement; Macronutrients: phosphorus, potassium, calcium, magnesium; Micronutrients: iron, manganese, zinc, copper; Cation exchange capacity; Organic matter content; Salinity and sodicity; and Soil texture class.

The test results will recommend optimal pH, nutritional ratios, and amounts of amendments needed based on your grass type and growth goals. For example, phosphorus is critical for new seedlings, but too much stresses mature lawns. Follow recommendations precisely. Understand each key parameter and how it impacts lawn health. pH outside the ideal range negatively affects nutrient availability. Excess or deficiency in primary macronutrients impairs growth. Low organic matter reduces water-holding capacity. Address out-of-range results methodically. The most common soil amendment suggested is the addition of lime to raise pH based on the overall alkalinity reading and desired pH for your turfgrass species. Lower pH negatively affects the availability of critical nutrients. Lime applications gradually neutralize acidity.

However, don't blindly apply lime per test results without considering current pH. Over-liming can swing pH too far alkaline. Limit lime applications even if the test recommends higher amounts if the current pH is acceptable for your grass type. Only apply enough to nudge pH into the ideal range.

Macronutrient deficiencies can be remedied by applying targeted fertilizer blends or organic amendments. For example, compost and manure add phosphorus, while sulfate of potash supplies potassium. Be patient in restoring key nutrients like phosphorus - follow a gradual multi-season approach.

Micronutrient shortages are best addressed through foliar sprays absorbing directly into grass leaf tissue. Soil applications are less effective for iron, manganese, and other micronutrients. Use a soluble chelated formulation and spray when grass is dry to avoid leaf burn.

Improving low organic matter requires a long-term plan of soil amendments to support microbial activity. Compost, peat, and natural mulch incorporated incrementally will raise organic content over time. Ensure future trimming and leaves are left to break down rather than removed.

Ideally, retest the soil after 1-2 seasons of adhering to recommendations to gauge progress. Persistence is needed to correct chronically deficient soil nutrients. Realize a single heavy application fails to remedy most issues - a light, steady approach brings sustained improvement.

While applying amendments, keep tracking lawn health visually for positive responses. Soil nutrients are just one factor in plant performance, along with sunlight, pests, irrigation, and the environment. Customize applications based on actual grass vigor.

Overall, a quality soil test provides invaluable insights that inform your fertilization, amendment, and pH adjustment practices. Combined with proper sampling technique and measured application of recommended products, you can transform the health of your soil and lawn.

3.2 pH Adjustments

While many factors influence lawn health, maintaining the proper pH range is crucial for the availability of essential nutrients. pH outside ideal ranges causes nutrient lockup and grass failure. Monitoring and amending pH ensures healthy growth.

The term pH refers to the acidity or alkalinity of soil based on a scale from 0-14, with seven neutral. Below seven is acidic, and above is alkaline. Most grasses thrive best between pH 6-7.5, with an ideal range depending on the variety. Soil testing determines the current pH.

Low pH causes essential nutrients like nitrogen, phosphorus, potassium, calcium, and magnesium to become locked up in insoluble compounds that roots cannot access. Manganese and iron reach excess toxic levels at low pH. Liming raises pH into the optimal range.

High pH above 7.5 triggers iron, manganese, boron, copper, and zinc deficiencies, making them unavailable despite soil presence. Excess sodium bicarbonates and carbonates drive alkalinity. Acidifying amendments lower high pH if needed.

While pH preference varies between grass species, cool-season grasses generally target a slightly acidic pH of 6.3-6.8. Warm-season zoysia and Bermuda thrive up to pH 7.4. Correcting pH too far beyond a grass' favored range causes issues.

The most common amendment for elevating pH is agricultural lime made from calcium carbonate. Dolomitic lime adds magnesium. Limedissolves slowly over months, so apply well before the growing season for availability. Follow soil test recommendations.

Lowering overly alkaline pH creates soil acidity through microbial activity using elemental sulfur products. The process is gradual - apply sulfur in the fall to effect the next growing season. Use only when truly justified by soil test results.

Liquid soil acidifiers using natural organic acids offer faster pH drops than lime or sulfur. However, effects are transient compared to permanent mineral amendments. Use liquid acids only as a short-term treatment.

Regular retesting determines soil pH maintenance needs over the years. Fluctuations happen over time based on rain, fertilizer use, decomposition, and leaching. Adjust pH incrementally through light, regular applications, not massive individual doses.

Proper pH improves nutrient efficiency for healthy growth, disease resistance, and rooting vigor. Combined with tailored fertility programs based on soil tests, keep your lawn's pH in its ideal comfort zone for performance and appeal. When applying any pH adjustment, proper fertilizer application techniques are key for success. Follow soil test recommended rates precisely and apply amendments during active grass growth, not dormancy. Distribute products evenly using calibrated spreaders and irrigate after application to dissolve and incorporate amendments into the soil. Avoid applying directly to grass foliage due to potential leaf burn. Retest pH after several months to gauge effectiveness and adjust future application rates based on tailored lawn needs.

Additionally, several secondary practices influence pH balance over time that must be accounted for. Regular liming and fertilization often cause pH to decline gradually, requiring monitoring and adjustment:some weed killers and insecticides also lower pH as a side effect. Heavy turf use from foot traffic or mowing removes alkalinity over years of harvest. Consider these dynamics in your overall turf management program when planning pH adjustments.

Low soil pH significantly below six can sometimes be ameliorated by increasing organic matter through compost, manure, or peat applications before liming. Organics provide pH buffering, but their effects are mild and temporary. For permanent neutralizing of acidity, proper liming is essential at the rates recommended by testing.

Rapid pH shifts induce grass stress, whether too acidic or alkaline. Make incremental changes gradually over 1-2 years, not through instant over-correction. This patience allows grass and soil microbial ecosystems time to adapt to the new pH environment. Areas of bare soil and thin turf are most vulnerable to burn after amendments, so focus initial applications on thicker established turf sections. Grass started from new seed should wait many months before altering pH.

3.3 Weed Control Methods

Weeds compete with desirable grass for space, light, water, and nutrients. Left unchecked, weeds diminish lawn health, function, and beauty. Integrating proper weed control builds better turfgrass by managing unwanted plants.

The best weed control starts with robust lawn management, fostering thick consistent growth and recovery. Healthy lawns resist weeds naturally. But chemical and mechanical treatments also play vital roles in maintaining clean turfgrass.

Preemergent herbicides prevent the germination of weed seeds already in the soil. Whenapplied before the warm-season grass green-up and thecool-season spring growth, preemergents provide 3-5 months of control for reduced weeding later. Non-selective preemergents control all seedlings.

Post emergent herbicides target actively growing weeds after they sprout. Selective post emergents only kill specific weeds, while non-selective glyphosate products kill all plant types, including lawn grass. Careful application timing and coverage are crucial for post emergents.

Surfactants added to post emergent sprays enable better absorption into weed leaf surfaces. Add according to product labels when mixing for maximum effectiveness. Avoid herbicide application to drought-stressed turf and when daytime air temperatures exceed 85°F.

Granular pre and post emergent herbicide products give longer residual control versus liquid forms. Granules need irrigation or rainfall for activation. Liquid sprays act faster but have shorter protection windows. Granular weed control offers flexibility in application timing.

When using herbicides, always carefully follow label instructions for rate, spray volume, nozzle type, and pressure. Misapplication risks lawn damage or failure to control weeds. Repeat treatments on a schedule based on the label for duration of control.

Rotate using different product active ingredients over the years to prevent weed resistance. For example, alternate preemergents between prodiamine and dithiopyr season to season. Combining multiple products also increases the control spectrum.

Hand pull small outbursts of perennial weeds like dandelions with a soil knife, removing all roots to prevent regrowth. Pull weeds early before they seed and spread. Spot treat isolated weed patches rather than entire lawns. Follow up with preemergents.

For severe crabgrass and clover infestations, renovation including tillage and re-seeding provides a fresh start. Tilling buries weed seeds too deep to thrive. Re-seed with quality grass varieties resistant to future weed encroachment. Corn gluten meal provides an organic preemergent control option derived from corn protein. It suppresses weed seed germination without chemicals for those seeking natural methods. However, corn gluten does not kill emerged weeds.

Vinegar-based sprays can eliminate young broadleaf weeds after sprouting. Concentrations of 5-20% acetic acid damage weed foliage but dissipate quickly, requiring reapplication. Avoid vinegars touching desired lawn grass. Horticultural vinegar is most effective but must be used cautiously.

Whatever weed control products are chosen, proper application technique is vital for safety and performance. Calibrate spreaders and sprayers precisely based on label rates. Time granular applications for rain or watering activation. Follow label information about required protective equipment.

Maintaining a dense weed-free turf stand starts with good cultural practices supporting lawn health and recovery. Integrate aeration, overseeding, fertilization, and proper mowing with selective herbicide use as the basis for preventing weed issues.

Tolerating some low-growth weeds is an option if they are not compromising lawn health and function. For example, allowing clover in low amounts supplies nitrogen and requires less water while filling bare patches where grass struggles. Complete weed elimination is not always required.

Weed control and healthy grass culture must be compatible.. Avoid overusing preemergents year after year, preventing desirable grass seed germination and rooting. Use a balanced approach tailored to specific lawn weed challenges.

Monitor and record weed outbreaks yearly to understand patterns and focus control appropriately. For example, repeat yellow nutsedge in wet zones signals a drainage issue to correct. Adjust maintenance practices contributing to weed colonization.

No single product or treatment universally controls all weed types in all situations. Integrate multiple mechanical, cultural, and chemical tactics as conditions warrant. Proper weed identification ensures targeting vulnerabilities of specific invading plants. Persistence is key to sustainable results.

3.4 Insect Treatments

Like weeds, insect pests compete with and damage turfgrass plants. Effective insect controls prevent deterioration from common lawn invaders like grubs, ants, chinchbugs, and others when infestations overwhelm natural defenses.

The best insect prevention starts with maintaining optimal lawn growing conditions. Healthy, vigorous grass can better withstand moderate pest pressure without significant loss. But thresholds often demand treatment to avoid decimation.

For any insect outbreak, start by accurately identifying the species and learning its life cycle. This allows timing controls to vulnerable stages and preferred food sources. Quick identification also avoids wasting time and chemicals on the wrong targets.

For some pests like grubs and chinchbugs, highly effective preventative control products are applied before damage is visible. These residual chemicals kill pests emerging later in peak season. Well-timed preventative treatments are critical.

Curative treatments are applied after pest detection when active damage is occurring. These target existing insects versus future generations. Curative controls typically have faster knockdown but shorter protection windows versus preventatives.

Insecticide classes include contact killers absorbed through the exterior skeleton for a quick knockdown and systemic chemicals taken up internally, providing longer residual control as pests feed. Rotate among classes for resistance prevention.

Granular formulations provide excellent residual activity and efficient coverage for preventative root and soil pests like grubs and ants. Carefully calibrate and apply early according to species lifecycles. Irrigate lightly after application.

For foliar feeders like caterpillars, liquid sprays allow targeted application only where pests are present. Use coarse, low-pressure droplets for controlling coverage on grass leaf surfaces. Repeat treatments are often needed.

When using any insecticide, carefully review and follow label directions for protective equipment, application directions, storage, and disposal. Measure rates accurately based on species, infestation levels, and turfgrass maturity. Natural and organic insecticide options include bio-insecticides like Bacillus thuringiensis (Bt) bacteria, neem oil extracts, insecticidal soaps, and plant-derived pyrethroids like pyrethrin. Though not as immediately powerful, these alternatives can be repeated frequently while minimizing chemical exposure and effects on lawns.

Toxicity to pollinators should always be part of the insecticide selection criteria. Many affect bees negatively to some degree, but neonicotinoids like imidacloprid are particularly dangerous to bees and other beneficial insects. Avoid applying such products to lawns and gardens when pollinators are active.

Beyond conventional chemical controls, several cultural practices can reduce insect pest pressure in lawns. Maintaining turf health through proper mowing height, fertilization, and watering avoids stress, making it vulnerable. Reducing excessive thatch deprives shelter habitat for some insects.

Likewise, properly maintaining nearby trees through conservative pruning, nutrition, and avoiding mechanical injury deters harmful tree pests from moving to lawns as alternate food sources when weakened. Keeping trees healthy provides benefits well beyond the trees themselves for integrated pest control.

If applying insecticide as a curative measure, use a separate mower and avoid removing clippings immediately after spraying to prevent accidentally transporting chemicals outside the lawn. Leave or compost affected clippings in place.

Alternate insecticide classes and products over seasons and avoid overuse of any single chemical. Rotating controls help prevent resistance in local insect populations from developing. Varied rotation also broadens the pest types controlled.

For ongoing insect challenges, enroll a lawn care company or DIY service on a preventative insecticide program, applying treatments at the proper calendar timing for your region. Preventative plans often prove more effective and affordable than repeated curative applications after infestations are rampant each year. But ensure the company has strong technical expertise.

No single product addresses all possible lawn insects in all situations. Continually monitor the lawn for early detection of harmful pest outbreaks. Be prepared to apply targeted curative treatments promptly at the first signs of trouble before extensive damage occurs. A combination of vigilant early intervention and proactive prevention provides the best turfgrass insect control.

3.5 Disease Prevention

Like all plants, turfgrass is susceptible to fungal, bacterial, and viral diseases under certain conditions. Infected lawns display symptoms like discoloration, lesions, decay, and dieback. Integrated disease controls prevent major outbreaks, preserving lawn health.

The most important disease prevention strategy is cultivating healthy grass through proper cultural practices. Vigorous lawns resist and recover from pathogens better than stressed, weakened turf. Ensure optimal fertility, soil, sunlight, and water to minimize disease vulnerability.

Excessive nitrogen fertility stimulates succulent blade growth, which is vulnerable to fungi. Apply balanced slow-release fertilizers to avoid surges in growth and maintain carbohydrate reserves. Allow soil to dry adequately between watering and provide good drainage.

Dethatching helps remove the damp mat layer where many fungal organisms thrive. Aerate to improve soil oxygen levels. Both combat the conditions most fungi need. Adjust irrigation to avoid prolonged wetness on leaf surfaces.

When diseases like brown patch and Pythium appear, avoid disrupted mowing and leaf damage, which spreads infection. Adjust to maximum cutting height and sharpen blades for clean cuts. Bag and remove clippings from affected areas.

Early detection and identification of diseases allow matching treatments to pathogens. Symptoms that resemble drought stress or insect damage may actually stem from unrecognized diseases. Accurate diagnosis guides suitable fungicide selection.

Once identified, follow label rates and directions closely for any fungicide or bactericide application. Use proper protective equipment and avoid drift. Target the treatments only where disease is present to minimize exposure. Rotate chemical classes for resistance prevention.

Preventative systemic fungicide products absorbed into grass plants offer 1-2 months of protection from future infection. These are ideal before peak disease seasons. Curative fungicides act faster on existing infections but have a shorter control duration.

Biological fungicides contain benign bacteria that outcompete pathogens for space and nutrients when applied early before extensive infection. These provide moderate control without chemical residues or risks. Reapply frequently for effect. Cultural controls like leaf blowing to promote air circulation and reduce foliage moisture also deter disease naturally. Allow grass plants time to dry thoroughly between irrigations. Prompt mowing removal of diseased leaf blades limits spread.

For chronic or severe disease issues, turf varietal resistance should guide the next grass selection. Mixing multiple resistant cultivars also provides a hedge against future epidemics. Contact local extension agents for advice on disease-resilient varieties proven in your area and conditions.

Masking disease symptoms with quick green-up sprays is never a permanent solution. Determine and address the underlying conditions enabling disease rather than temporary symptom-hiding fixes. However, pigment products limit damage between treatment applications when disease flares up.

During any fungicide or pesticide application, use hoses and low-pressure nozzles to avoid spraying chemical mists that may drift. Water in products after application to prevent runoff. Safely discard excess mixed chemicals - never reuse the last tank remnants in the next session.

Keep accurate records of fungal disease outbreaks, treatments, timing, and results, detailing which products and application methods proved most effective or ineffective. Refine your disease prevention plans yearly based on this history to maximize effect.

Enrolling with a lawn care company offering routine fungicide prevention programs takes the guesswork out of product selection and timing. But ensure the company has regional experience with the specific disease issues you aim to prevent. Do-it-yourself control is also very achievable with proper planning.

While conventional fungicides remain important tools, continue enhancing lawn health between applications through non-chemical means of improving drainage, reducing irrigation, proper fertilization, mowing adjustments, or overseeding thin areas. Strong turfgrass is your ally against diseases.

A combination of vigilant scouting for early disease detection, prompt targeted application of proven fungicide products, and diligent cultural practices to promote turf health provide the most effective and sustainable disease control over the long term. Preventative care shields lawns from extensive crippling damage.

3.6 Lawn Alternative Options

While lush turfgrass lawns remain popular for yards, increasing interest in reduced maintenance and sustainability has driven the adoption of alternative landscapes using hardscapes, native plants, edibles, and more. Rethinking traditional lawns offers options better suited for certain conditions, and priorities.

Homeowners, businesses, municipalities and even golf courses are shrinking excessive grass areas requiring significant upkeep. Replacing turf with walkways, patios, decking, mulched beds, rock gardens, and low-growing native groundcovers provides eye-appealing replacements with major water, chemical and maintenance savings.

Jamie Tukey

Many properties contain expansive low-use lawn spaces along borders, on embankments, under dense shade, or in unused sections, receiving little enjoyment yet demanding care. Converting these fringe zones to alternative landscaping is an easy first step to reducing unrewarding lawn maintenance.

For play areas needing durable traffic-resistant surfaces, synthetic turf offerings have advanced greatly from older generations. Quality artificial lawns now mimic natural grass in appearance and feel, but without mowing, irrigation, fertilizer, or pest issues. Advanced drainage and antimicrobial properties improve performance.

Likewise, vegetable and ornamental gardens offer functionality and color diversity beyond a monoculture lawn. Herb varieties can complement cookouts with fresh garnish picked on demand. Flower beds that bloom in sequence provide recurring pops of color and curb appeal. Edible landscaping options are expanding rapidly.

A reduced lawn also means less mowing, fuel use, emissions, and noise. Replacing grass along prominent borders with low groundcovers, gravel, or mulch showcases the home while eliminating trimming needs. Limit lawn to functional spaces only.

Native plants specially adapted to local climate and soils require far less maintenance once established. Their deep root systems access moisture and nutrients more independently. Site-appropriate native mixes thrive naturally with little intervention. If reducing high water demand is a priority, xeriscaping with drought-tolerant native plants is ideal for drier climates. Varieties range from succulents and ornamental grasses to flowering perennials. Site soil preparation is key, along with proper mulching and irrigation during establishment.

Some lawn conversions utilize a hybrid approach, integrating pockets of synthetic turf, patios, and small remaining live turf areas into aesthetically pleasing mini-scapes. This balances usability for recreation with ultra-low maintenance options. Families design customized combinations matching their needs.

If retaining any lawn area, ensure the underlying irrigation system technology supports water conservation. Smart controllers, high-efficiency nozzles, drip zones, and moisture sensor activation precisely match real water needs rather than wasted overwatering.

When renovating turf for new landscape uses, call 811 for buried utility line locating before any excavation or trenching. Removing old grass also provides an ideal opportunity to improve soil, drainage, and subsurface conditions through amendments before installing replacement plants or materials.

Seek advice from qualified landscape designers when planning significant lawn conversions. Experts can suggest ideal plant varieties, hardscapes, and layouts tailored to your specific conditions and preferences. Local extension offices also provide guidance on regional plant selections.

Lawn alternatives provide exciting possibilities, but research maintenance needs for any plantings. Some appear simple initially but require eventual pruning, fertilization, and care comparable to turfgrass. Assess long-term commitments realistically when evaluating options.

If converting side or back lawn spaces, ensure sufficient paved access remains for lawn care equipment to reach any remaining turf areas. Creating inaccessible islands of grass should be avoided. Also, consider impacts on children's play areas when resizing lawns.

Rethinking traditional expanses of lawn grass opens possibilities for diverse, sustainable landscapes that better match needs and conditions. But reductions should balance aesthetics and purpose. Blend the lawn with water-wise plants, hardscapes, and synthetic turf for maximum benefit.

55

Chapter 4
Seasonal Lawn Care

4.1 Spring Lawn Preparation

The arrival of spring provides an opportunity to remedy winter damage and set your lawn up for success as the growing season kicks off. Key spring preparations include clearing debris, assessing conditions, aerating, overseeding, fertilizing, and adjusting mowing practices.

Start spring lawn care by removing leaves, sticks, and other accumulated debris. Rake thoroughly or utilize a mower with a bagging attachment to lift flattened material and allow air circulation to the soil. Remove any protective matting that was used over winter.

Inspect the lawn closely, looking for dead patches needing spot repair. Rake back any matted grass layers to check for new growth underneath. Assess leftover winter weed presence like chickweed and henbit. Target the early preemergent herbicide applications.

Spring is prime time for core aeration, while soil moisture is ample before the summer heat arrives. Aeration relieves winter soil compaction and promotes drainage and root growth as grass greens up. Dethatching prior clears the way for better tine penetration if substantial mat buildup occures.

Overseed thin or bare areas to improve density, fill in divots from winter damage, and crowd out spring weeds. Rake and level the soil lightly before applying quality seed that is well matched for user conditions. Maintain consistent moisture while new the grass is established.

Apply starter fertilizer formulated explicitly for new spring growth and recovery after cold weather dormancy. Slow-release organic options work well to supply macronutrients for 2-3 months, avoiding growth surges from synthetic soluble fertilizers.

As consistent spring temperatures arrive and cool season grasses initiate flush new growth, it's time to begin mowing. Gradually reduce cutting height over several mowings until reaching the desired level for the grass species. Never remove more than 1/3 of the blade length when mowing.

Clean up prunings, fallen sticks, and other debris accumulated over lawn areas from nearby garden beds and trees during winter. Remove hazards before mowing operations commence. Compost healthy materials onsite or dispose of them responsibly offsite.

If possible, perform any renovation or expansion projects early while grass remains dormant. This reduces stress. Complete major overhauls before desired grass actively grows,and resume regularl watering and fertilizing once green-up is initiated.

Spring also brings the germination of summer annual weeds like crabgrass. Apply preemergent control early according to label directions to prevent future outbreaks. Time applications before soil temperatures reach 55 degrees Fahrenheit. Spring is the ideal time for soil testing and to apply any recommended lime or sulfur amendments needed to adjust pH based on results. Proper spring pH sets up nutrient availability for the entirel growing season. Send samples to a reputable lab.

Inspect any irrigation system components for damage or leaks from winter freezes. Perform maintenance on heads, valves, or timers so the system reliably operates when activated for the warmer season. Check the accessibility of the water source.

Sharpen mower blades after winter storage to ensure clean cuts that heal quickly. Replace any heavily worn or damaged blades that lack sharp edges. Properly balanced and angled blades prevent tearing and shredding during mowing operations.

Monitor soil moisture and rainfall in early spring. Water newly overseeded areas lightly and frequently to aid germination until sprouts are visible. Provide supplemental irrigation if precipitation lags. Gradually increase the depth between watering as roots develop.

Let the lawn naturally wake itself up in spring rather than forcing top growth too early through heavy fertilization. Allow soil temperatures to progressively warm before pushing top growth. Be patient while nature takes its course.

Spring is also prime time for crabgrass and other annual warm season grassy weed preemergent control. Get preemergent down before soil temperatures reach 55-60 F to prevent germination. Crabgrass springs up in thin lawns.

Stay off newly seeded areas initially to prevent seed displacement and soil compaction while grass is esablished. As the plants grow denser, light foot traffic can be tolerated. Avoid heavy use during the first full season to prevent damage.

Inspect trees, shrubs, and garden bed edges bordering the lawn for encroachment into turf areas. Redefine clean edges around beds so grass can fill back in fully up to the edge. Prune back intruding branches shading the lawn.

Don't lower mowing height excessively early in spring, even if the weather warms. Gradually reduce height over a span of 4-6 weeks, allowing grass blades to acclimate and build carbohydrate reserves slowly.

Proper spring preparations optimize conditions for vigorous lawn growth once temperatures consistently warm. Prioritize removal of debris, preemergent weed control, overseeding, PH adjustment, aeration, and careful mowing practices as your lawn exits dormancy.

4.2 Summer Lawn Maintenance

Summer's hot and often dry conditions bring additional lawn care needs to keep the grass healthy and vibrant despite stresses. Priorities include proper mowing, irrigation, pest control, and responding to problems promptly.

Raise mowing height during summer's peak temperatures to insulate crowns and roots from heat exposure and retain moisture longer. For cool-season grasses, move the height up 1 inch higher than the spring level. Cutting no lower than 3 inches is recommended.

Let grass grow longer between cuts, removing no more than 1/3 total of the blade length with each mowing session. This preserves carbohydrate reserves in the plants to sustain summer conditions. More frequent shallow mowing demands more energy from stressed turf.

Keep mower blades sharpened to reduce leaf tearing and water loss. Dull blades give a white shredded appearance rather than clean cuts. Sharpen after every 8-10 hours of use. Replace damaged blades to prevent imbalance problems.

Adjust irrigation run times and frequency for weather conditions, applying only enough to compensate for lack of rainfall. Avoid daily shallow watering, which trains roots to stay near the surface. Prioritize deep weekly soaking while allowing drying in between.

Monitor turf color and footprint indentations for visible indications of water needs before water stress sets in. Irrigate when 30-50% of blades show fold or roll. Use moisture sensors or probes to gauge soil condition at root level out of view.

Apply finer nutrient particles during hot weather to avoid foliar burn from granules. Light monthly doses of soluble nutrients stimulate growth and recovery for high-traffic lawns during peak growing seasons. Organic treatments elicit a slower response.

Scout constantly for pest or disease outbreaks when the grass is compromised in summer. Treat aggressively at first signs rather than allowing infestations to expand. Conditions prime for chinch bug, grubs, fungus, and drought stress damage require vigilance.

Adjust expectations for turf color and density compared to cooler seasons. Prioritize health and vigor over ideal appearance. Support growth through proper nutrition and rainfall without pushing excessive growth that demands added mowing. Avoid mowing when the grass is wet or heat-stressed—clip only in the morning or late evening when cool and dry. Wet blades clump under the mower deck and lead to an uneven cut. Midday mowing causes excess transpiration.

Apply grub control products in early summer according to local schedules to prevent damage from actively feeding insects later in the season. Confirm application timing for your specific area and pest issues.

Monitor automatic irrigation systems to ensure proper coverage without any missed areas or blocked heads. Make adjustments to reach far corners fully. Repair any leaks promptly to conserve water.

In drought-prone regions, allow the lawn to gradually enter dormancy during extended hot and dry periods if needed. Dormant grass crowns will remain alive and recover upon renewed rainfall while attempting to irrigate excessively risks long-term damage.

Reduce foot traffic in stressed or struggling areas to prevent further injury. Temporarily keep people and pets off sections needing an opportunity to recover. Prevent soil compaction and physical damage to grass plants.

Control broadleaf summer weeds like spurge with selective herbicides after spot-treating bare or thinning areas with seed to fill gaps. Allow newly seeded grass to establish before applying chemicals. Follow label directions closely.

Avoid spraying herbicides during extreme heat when weeds are stressed. Products optimally function when applied in cooler temperatures with adequate soil moisture present. Monitor weather forecasts when scheduling applications.

Condition and amend lawn soil mid-summer if renovating in fall. Add lime if needed to adjust pH, incorporate quality compost, aerate, and potentially apply gypsum if soils are compacted. Ready the soil for new grass.

For warm-season grasses, time summer pre-emergent herbicide applications around June 1st to control annual bluegrass and ryegrass emerging in fall. For cool-season lawns, hold off until August when soils cool.

Schedule core aeration in early summer to improve drought tolerance. Pulling plugs enables better water penetration and retention in the root zone. Making two passes perpendicular maximizes the benefit.

4.3 Fall Lawn Care

Fall brings ideal conditions to renovate and fortify cool-season lawns before winter dormancy. Essential fall practices include overseeding, fertilization, pest control, and mowing adjustments. Planning fall improvements sets up success when growth resumes next spring.

Fall is the best time to overseed thin, worn, or bare lawn areas. Air temperatures and soil moisture remain high while growth rates slow from summer peaks. This allows new grass seeds to germinate and establish roots before harsh weather.

Cool-season grasses like fescue should be overseeded roughly 6-8 weeks before expected first frost so plants develop hardened crowns. In warmer climates overseeding can extend later into fall. Time seeding in your area accordingly.

Before overseeding:
Mow, aerate, and dethatch to prepare a seedbed—work topsoil amendment into bare spots.
Apply starter fertilizer when seeding, then again after 4-6 weeks for continued fill-in.
Use care when mowing newly overseeded areas.

If planning complete lawn renovation, early fall allows time for kill-off, soil prep, seeding, and establishment of new grass before winter arrives. However, reseeding must occur at least 30 days before ground freezes for root development.

Where existing turf remains healthy, fertilize according to soil test guidance to strengthen grass before dormancy. Opt for slow-release organic sources feeding for 6-8 weeks. Avoid excess nitrogen stimulation prone to disease and failure to harden off properly.

Monitor for fall diseases like brown patches and Pythium during warm stretches. Treat any infection early and quickly to avoid lawn loss. Focus on prevention with proper cultural practices and targeted fungicide applications where warranted.

Schedule core aeration in early fall once night temperatures reliably cool back below 60° F. Aerate again perpendicular to the first pass for maximum benefit, opening the soil before winter sets in. Thatching before aerating enables better tine penetration if a substantial debris layer is present. Apply pre-emergent crabgrass control herbicide in early September for cool-season grasses. This prevents annual grassy weeds next year. The timing for warm-season lawns is spring. Use caution around new seedlings.

Raise mowing height for the final cuts of the season. Allow grass to grow slightly taller to insulate crowns from cold weather. Never cut more than 1/3 of the total blade length when mowing dormant grass. Continue mowing until growth fully stops.

Clean up fallen leaves regularly using a mulching mower or rake. Excessive leaf cover smothers grass. Compost leaves or dispose of them properly offsite if the volume exceeds mulching capacity. Chopped leaves can be left as a beneficial winter cover.

Continue irrigation into early fall but reduce frequency as growth slows, temperatures cool, and rainfall increases. Gradually toughen plants by allowing moderate drought stress before going dormant. Water any new seedings as needed for establishment.

In warmer regions, overseed with ryegrass in early fall for a lush green color throughout winter when typical grass species go dormant. The fast-growing ryegrass dies out as warm-season grasses green back up in spring.

Spot treat any persistent broadleaf or grassy weeds to prevent proliferation when grass enters dormancy. Target weeds when actively growing and avoid winds or excessive heat.

Schedule any planned lime applications at least six weeks before the expected ground freeze. This allows the lime adequate incorporation time to modify pH before spring. Follow soil test recommendations for product and application rate.

Use fall as an opportunity to improve lawn health through core aeration, overseeding, targeted fertilization, and weed control. Proper fall preparations translate into enhanced spring green-up.

4.4 Winterizing Your Lawn

Preparing lawns properly each fall ensures healthy grass and minimizes winter damage. Key winterizing steps include mowing adjustments, irrigation changes, fertilization, and protective coverings as warranted. Advance preparations avoid issues come spring.

Continue regular mowing at incrementally higher heights into late fall. Finish the season by cutting cool season grasses like fescue at 3-3.5 inches. Never remove more than 1/3 of the total blade length when mowing dormant turf.

Make the final mowing pass with blades sharpened for a clean cut. This avoids any damage or tears, increasing vulnerability to harsh weather. Dull blades shred leaf tips, leaving ragged edges. Touch-up blade sharpening just before winter.

Remove fallen leaves, sticks, and other debris using a mulching mower or rake during winter. Excessive accumulation can smother and damage grass. Leave chopped leaves as a protective winter mulch layer if less than an inch deep.

Discontinue irrigation systems after the final mowing when grass enters dormancy and rainfall increases. Bleed and drain above-ground supply pipes and backflow preventers to avoid freeze damage where applicable.

Apply winterizing fertilizer 6-8 weeks before the expected ground freeze to strengthen crowns before dormancy. Slow-release organic sources are preferable to avoid growth surges late in the season.

Protect irrigation system components like valves and backflow preventers from freeze damage by insulating, draining, and enclosing vulnerable elements. Confirm all water is off and supply openings sealed.

In warmer regions, overseeding thinly covered areas with fast-growing ryegrass in the fall provides a green winter color. The ryegrass dies when warm-season grasses green back up in spring. In regions with reliable winter snow cover, applying extra potassium in late fall strengthens grass cold tolerance. Potassium aids ice crystal formation in crowns, protecting them from freeze damage. Follow soil test recommendations for any deficient levels.

Reduce mowing frequency as growth slows through fall, but continue cutting until turf stops growing to avoid leaving long untrimmed blades over winter. Never cut dormant grass shorter than 2 inches for insulation.

Remove and empty hose bib filters and backflow preventers to avoid cracked components. Store them open and dry over winter. Ensure all shutoff valves are fully closed and isolated. Turn off and drain any irrigation system pumps and supply lines.

Perform pump service and maintenance for irrigation systems in the fall to avoid freezing weather issues. Replace worn seals, lubricate motors, and clear debris. Test operation and winterize well before hard freezes arrive.

For areas with reliable winter snow cover but fluctuating temperatures causing freeze and thaw cycles, apply anti-desiccant spray to crowns in early winter. This provides a protective coating preventing dehydration and winter kill.

Install temporary protective lawn coverings in far northern areas where minimal snow accumulation occurs. Use breathable material, allowing light and air penetration. Remove covers in early spring after final hard freezes.

Mow, dethatch, aerate, fertilize, and overseed according to grass type in early fall. But discontinue intensive practices after seeding to gradually allow grass to toughen before dormancy gradually. Avoid late surges in growth through excess care.

Schedule irrigation controller backflow device certification inspections as mandated before disconnecting and storing the controller over winter. Keep all inspection documentation current.

Properly winterizing your lawn in fal,l avoids many common problems come spring like weed infestations, desiccation, freeze damage, and pest vulnerability. Advance preparations maintain turf health and vigor across seasons.

4.5 Lawn Care Calendars

Following optimal timing for key lawn care activities ensures your grass thrives in every season. Create a customized lawn calendar reminding you when to aerate, seed, feed, prune, and maintain your specific turfgrass varieties based on your climate.

Tailor your calendar to warm-season grasses like Bermuda versus cool-season types such as fescue. Their seasonal growth patterns differ. Observe local university guidance for your grass and environment. For example, target pre-emergent crabgrass control around March 1 for fescue lawns in Kentucky but April 1 for Georgia.

While adaptations will be needed yearly with seasonal variations, maintain a master calendar for consistency from one year to the next. Record dates when you observe certain events, like the first flowering of forsythia or when lilac blooms have all dropped. Use these natural phenological signs as reminders to align activities annually.

In northern cool season lawns, concentrate efforts in fall for seeding and fortifying grass before winter. Time spring works like pre-emergents when forsythia blooms. Summer focuses on irrigation, growth regulation, and pest control. Fall readies the lawn for colder months again.

Transition zone lawns balancing cool and warm-season varieties need attention in spring, summer, and fall. Overseed bare spots in fall and spring as weather permits. Control summer weeds and pests aggressively. Maintain year-round color and function with proper timing.

In southern lawns, focus on readying warm season grasses to thrive in heat. Spring green-up, late summer overseeding, and pre-emergent winter weed control are pivotal. Ensure adequate mid-summer irrigation and nutrition. Work centers on supporting growth in the hottest periods.

Beyond seasonal care, build in standard intervals for key activities like mowing, fertilizing, aerating, and spraying. For example, plan to fertilize approximately every 6-8 weeks, aerate in early fall, inspect irrigation monthly, and dethatch every 1-2 years. Consistent, proactive care prevents problems.

No single ideal lawn calendar suits all users in a given area. Prioritize developing a customized schedule matching your specific environment, grass varieties, use patterns, and maintenance goals. Seek local guidance, but observe your lawn's needs closely, too. When creating your calendar, consult online resources and publications from local universities detailing optimal timing in your area. Base schedules on data from field research nearby rather than generic recommendations, and fine-tune dates as you gain experience.

Set calendar reminders on your smartphone or computer tied to specific lawn care tasks and target dates. Build in advance notifications such as two weeks prior so preparations can be made. Sync your lawn calendar to other household schedules and responsibilities.

Incorporate flexibility to adjust scheduled activities around weather conditions as needed. For example, postpone mowing after heavy rains or delay fertilizer application during droughts. Allow rescheduling to protect lawn health.

Keep prior years' maintenance logs and use them to tune calendar timing for each task. For instance, note actual dates when crabgrass first appeared to better time next year's pre-emergent herbicide application.

Carefully record pest outbreak dates, fertilization schedules, overseeding work, and other activities to make incremental improvements each year. Observe patterns and environmental factors influencing your lawn over time.

Leave space for additional follow-up applications that may be required if issues emerge. For example, schedule a follow-up fungicide treatment two weeks after the initial application to combat the spread of diseases like brown patch. Expect multiple treatments for some issues.

When scheduling annual core aeration, factor in renting or accessing the necessary equipment, and book well in advance of planned sessions to ensure availability. The same may apply to dethatching equipment or other specialized machinery.

However, system will perfectly forecast seasonal variability from year to year. But investing in an organized lawn care calendar tailored to your environment will keep your turfgrass looking its best and save money through proper timing.

4.6 Regional Considerations

While following core lawn care principles, some practices require adjustment for unique regional characteristics across North America. Tailor your lawn maintenance calendar, accounting for climate, soil, pests, and other local factors influencing grass performance.

Northern cool season lawns experience a concentrated growing season in spring and fall bracketed by harsh winters. Focus efforts on fall overseeding for recovery before the ground freezes. Apply a balanced fertilizer in early fall, low in nitrogen. Maintain mowing into late fall until growth entirely stops.

Transition zone climates support both cool and warm-season grasses. Overseed thinly covered areas in fall and spring as weather allows. Control heavy summer weed and insect pressure in the heat. Foster year-round green color through proper variety mixing and scheduling.

Southern lawns emphasize warm-season grasses like Bermuda and zoysia. Time spring and early summer pre-emergent weed treatments around March-April to control crabgrass and other invaders before heat arrives. Prioritize summer fertility and pest management. Water deeply and infrequently.

West region residents combat arid conditions, water restrictions, and alkaline soils. Seek low-water grasses like buffalograss or improved tall fescues. Amend irrigation use and frequencies for conservation: test and correct high soil pH levels. Reduce large lawns not functionally used.

In coastal zones, salt-tolerant varieties help withstand saline soils and sea spray. Improved Bermuda cultivars thrive despite soil and airborne salt exposure. Adjust mowing and fertility to support recovery from occasional hurricane damage using prudent fertilizer practices.

Great Plains states face extreme cold, wind desiccation, and periods of heat and drought. Allow grass to acclimate slowly in spring and fall. Water deeply and monitor for pests when moisture deficient. Ensure soil nutrient testing includes micronutrients like sulfur prone to leaching.

Pacific Northwest areas deal with fungal issues in persistently damp and moderate temperatures. Emphasize aeration and dethatching to dry soils while avoiding over-watering. Introduce fast-drying intergrade fescue cultivars. Control moss aggressively before extensive infestation. Northeastern states experience cold winters, ample rainfall, short springs, and moderate summers. Concentrate on fall overseeding and fortification before winter. Raise mowing heights gradually as growth slows in fall. Apply lime well before ground freeze for proper pH modification by spring.

Mid-Atlantic areas target early fall pre-emergent control of summer annual grasses and broadleaf weeds emerging as the weather cools. Transition to warm-season grasses in southern zones while favoring cool-season types further north. Monitor for aggressive crabgrass and diseases.

Southeast lawns require vigilant insect and disease prevention in warm, humid conditions. Maintain good drainage and avoid overwatering. Reduce fertilizer amounts given ample rainfall and soil fertility. Use raised mowing heights for heat insulation and moisture retention.

High-altitude mountain regions have short growing periods between cold seasons. Work quickly in spring and fall when temps allow growth. Prioritize early fall feeding and fortification. Use faster establishing grasses on slopes prone to erosion. Control rodent issues over winter.

Urban lawns sustain heavier use and more reflected heat. Seek wear and drought-tolerant grass varieties. Increase mowing heights, aerate routinely, and dethatch to alleviate soil compaction. Monitor for dog urine burn and repetitive wear patterns.

In all regions, familiarize yourself with local university turfgrass research on ideal selections and practices proven to succeed in your specific environment. No general recommendations can replace this local real-world data for your unique growing conditions.

While following sound cultural practices universally, be ready to adapt schedules, varieties, amendments, and turf products to align with the strengths and weaknesses of your distinct region. Customizing your calendar maximizes lawn success.

Chapter 5
Lawn Care Tools & Equipment

5.1 Mower Options

Selecting the right mower for your lawn's size and features ensures you can maintain the turf properly and efficiently. Compare different mower types based on cutting width, power options, terrain capacities, and special features to choose the best model for your needs.

Gas-powered rotary mowers work well for typical residential lawns under 1/4 acre. Their spinning horizontal blades provide most grasses with a clean cut and mulching capability. Mid-size, 21-22 inch, widths suit small to medium yards. Self-propelled models reduce pushing effort for hilly or dense turf.

A riding mower offers efficient coverage for larger yards or semi-regular mowing of adjacent lots. Decks up to 42 inches wide significantly reduce mowing time compared to walk-behind units. Riding mowers are easy to use on slopes or large open areas. Higher-end models include turning radius for tighter spaces.

Electric and battery-powered mowers provide zero emissions operation compared to gas models. Corded electric mowers have unlimited run time but maneuverability limited by the cord length. Newer cordless battery models allow full mobility but run times under an hour. Battery technology continues improving.

Gasoline engine reliability, power, and convenient refueling give most homeowners the versatility needed for lawn maintenance. Look for modern 4-cycle engines meeting emissions standards and fuel efficiency technologies like auto choke shutoff.

Those with primarily flat terrain may find a traditional push reel mower ideal. The human-powered cutting from blades sliding past each other creates no emissions and little noise. Push models give exercise and save fuel costs. Larger yards require self-propelled reel models.

Tractor-style riding mowers allow adding attachments like pull-behind core aerators, dethatchers, or sprayers to enhance lawn care capacity with the same engine investment. Such multi-use tractors offer versatility but require storage space. Determine needed attachments when selecting.

Check manufacturer warranties and rated lifespans when purchasing. Units with steel decks and nam- brand engines hold up longer. Weigh aftermarket part availability. Carefully following use and maintenance guidelines extends the mower's lifespan significantly. Compare deck construction between models - rugged steel decks last considerably longer than aluminum or synthetics before needing replacement. Steel handles occasional impacts without major damage. Lighter deck materials dent more easily over time.

Higher horsepower does not necessarily equate to better cutting performance. Excessive power on lighter decks can lift the mower during cutting, producing an uneven finish. Ensure power levels match the intended deck size and thickness.

When possible, test demo models at dealership lots to assess comfort, maneuverability, and cutting results firsthand. Review how intuitive the controls are and the ease of settings adjustment. Ask about dealership maintenance specials.

Mulching and bagging attachments allow managing clippings differently for each mow. Side discharge areas create clumping rows needing re-distribution. Mulching kits conserve nutrients, and bagging aids the leaf debris cleanup.

Mower features like washout ports, anti-rust coatings, and sealed bearings extend lifespan in wet conditions. Padded adjustable handles reduce vibration. Quick height adjusters make setting changes easier between jobs.

For homeowners seeking professional-style cuts, reel mowers with fixed spinning blades provide the cleanest cut. But they require level terrain and frequent mowing. They are best for lawns under one acre and target those desiring an immaculate cut.

Maintain mower engines properly regardless of type for performance and longevity. Replace air, fuel, and oil filters regularly. Keep air intakes and cooling fins cleared of debris buildup. Sharpen and balance blades after each season.

Choosing the optimal mower for your specific combination of lawn size, terrain, obstacles, and usage needs saves time, ensures safety, and produces better turfgrass results. Invest in quality construction and components that will deliver reliability long-term.

5.2 Irrigation Systems

In many regions, an in-ground irrigation system is essential for convenient lawn watering without the hassles of hoses or sprinklers. Choose components wisely during planning and installation to ensure an efficient system providing adequate coverage.

Consider an automatic controller allowing custom watering schedules for each zone rather than timed models. Smart controllers integrate weather data and soil moisture sensor input to irrigate precisely as needed. These conserve water compared to timed cycling.

Spray heads and rotors determine water distribution across zones. Use consistent head types for even coverage. Sprays work well for smaller areas like borders, while larger rotors cover expansive zones. Distance, angles, and adjustable arc settings modulate overlap.

Combine head and nozzle choices to match precipitation rates across zones. Multi-stream multi-trajectory nozzles in rotors provide better water delivery than outdated single stream. Match the gallonage rates to your soil type and infiltration capacity.

Drip irrigation kits effectively water beds, trees, and slopes while reducing evaporation. Micro-spray heads attach along the hose for targeted small-area coverage. Underground drip runs under mulch for zone isolation. These significantly reduce overall water usage.

The piping network diameter size supports volume capacity to supply simultaneous zones reliably. One-inch lines often suffice for residential systems, but high demand needs larger mains. Consult an irrigation contractor for proper pipe sizing.

Automate system drain and winterization steps using compressed air blow-out kits. These will clear all lateral pipes and heads of standing water reliably without tedious manual draining. Installation options exist for new and existing systems.

Routine maintenance keeps systems operating optimally. Flush the lines annually to clear accumulated silt, minerals and debris. Adjust or replace worn nozzles, seals, and gaskets causing leaks. Keep heads vertical and unblocked by overgrowth. Select quality components at initial installation for long-term reliability. Specify reputable brands of piping like PVC over cheaper thin-walled polypipe prone to breaks. Use self-draining valve boxes to prevent freeze damage to anti-siphon valves.

Program multiple start times overnight for each zone to maximize absorption and minimize evaporation loss. Apply at slow rates matching soil infiltration capability. Cycle times generally range from 15-60 minutes per zone, depending on lawn size.

Consider installing a rain sensor that automatically delays watering after local precipitation. Alternatively, smart controllers utilize local weather feeds to avoid overwatering from natural rainfall. These reduce waste significantly.

In drought-prone areas, buried deeper lateral pipes prevent surface rooting for greater drought tolerance. Deep pipe placement encourages roots to grow deeper, seeking available subsoil moisture. This increases lawn resilience when rainfall is sparse.

Careful head placement avoids spraying impervious areas like roads and sidewalks, which wastes water to runoff. Position heads to conserve water while maximizing lawn coverage. Utilize curbless edging where possible.

Micro-irrigation through low-volume devices often exempts homeowners from irrigation restrictions. Reduce fines by switching to high-efficiency heads applying less than 30 gallons annually per sq ft if limits are imposed.

Ensure backflow prevention devices are installed and tested where local codes require. Such valves prevent contaminated water from flowing backward into home supply lines when irrigation systems activate.

Mark the position of lateral pipes and wiring with tracer wire for future reference when performing yard projects to avoid accidental line cuts. Also, have lines professionally located and marked through national Call Before You Dig services.

A quality in-ground irrigation system supplemented with smart technologies and zoned for specific lawn needs provides convenience while optimizing water use efficiency. Invest wisely during design and component selection for the best value long-term.

5.3 Aerators and Dethatchers

Core aerators and dethatching machines effectively improve soil structure and remove debris obstructing lawn health. The tow behind models are convenient for homeowners and simply attach to most standard riding or push mowers.

Core aerators puncture small holes into the soil profile to relieve compaction and improve drainage. Plug sizes under 0.75 inches wide help grass recover quickly. Aerators utilize coring tines mounted on heavy rolling drums. More tines penetrate deeper for better aeration.

For optimal penetration, choose an aerator with adjustable tine length settings. This increases depth gradually in multiple passes to extract cores thoroughly from heavily compacted soils if needed. Preset fixed tine models lack this incremental control.

Look for models with front caster and rear drive wheels supporting the frame rather than single axle units. The 4-point stability keeps the frame level and tines vertica,l preventing veering on slopes for clean, uniform holes.

While manual push aerators suitable for small yards exist, motorized tow units work far more efficiently in larger areas. Electric and gasoline engine models provide power to propel and operate the lifting action, reducing manual exertion.

Power take off (PTO) models designed for tractors offer three-point hitches for stable attachment and convenient raising or lowering by the tractor hydraulics between passes. However, PTO operation requires a suitable tractor with a compatible hitch setup.

Dethatching units also attach to standard ride-on or push mower in place of the cutting deck to remove debris from turfgrass. Blades, tines, or powered rakes comb into the lawn surface, collecting dead grass and roots into clippings.

Powered dethatcher models provide rotating tines or stiff bristled brushes that actively scrub and lift matted material from the lawn far more effectively than passive rakes. More forceful debris removal restores proper soil contact and aeration.

Tow-behind lawn maintenance attachments like aerators and dethatchers offer an affordable option for homeowners to perform critical lawn services themselves without the hassle of renting machinery or hiring contract work. Hitches allow swapping implements easily across the maintenance season. Sturdy steel construction ensures lasting value from the investment. Proper aeration and dethatching are essential components of a comprehensive lawn care program. While regular mowing, irrigation, and fertilization maintain healthy grass day-to-day and week-to-week, core aeration and thatch removal are periodic practices that promote long-term soil health and vigor. Using quality equipment matched to the size of your lawn, along with proper timing and technique, makes aerating and dethatching more effective. This section explores the major types of aerators and power rakes, how to use them correctly, optimal timing, and the many benefits you can expect from performing annual aeration and dethatching.

Core aeration involves extracting small plugs of soil from the lawn, leaving behind holes that allow air, water, and nutrients to penetrate deeper into the root zone. This helps alleviate soil compaction and encourages the grass plants to develop deeper, more extensive root systems. The soil cores break down over time, naturally refilling the holes. Manual core aerators use simple lever-activated tines to pull the plugs from the lawn. They require more physical exertion but work fine for smaller yards. Gas-powered or electric-driven aerators greatly reduce the labor needed, making them preferable for larger lawns. The plugs removed are typically 2-3 inches deep and 0.5-0.75 inches across. Recommended spacing is about 2-4 inches between holes. The more holes per given area, the better. Many aerators allow adjusting the tine depth and hole spacing. Always aerate when the soil is moist but not saturated, as overly wet soil is prone to compaction when aerated. Let the cores dry out and crumble before mowing again. Watering after aerating accelerates the breakdown of plugs.

Thatch is a spongy layer of accumulated grass stems, roots, and other organic matter that builds up when the rate of debris accumulation outpaces its decomposition. Power rakes, also called dethatchers, use rotating tines to aggressively lift and tear away this thatchy mat. Vertical cutting units slice through the thatch less invasively without disturbing the soil surface. When thatch depth approaches a half inch, it's time to dethatch, usually an annual task best performed in early fall. Adjust the tine depth carefully to avoid digging into the soil. Making multiple passes perpendicular to each other ensures more thorough thatch removal. Allow the lawn to dry before mowing and irrigating after dethatching or power raking. Overseeding right after taking advantage of the bare soil and enhanced seed-to-soil contact.

There are numerous benefits gained from performing core aeration and dethatching. Aeration physically removes plugs of soil, creating channels that alleviate compaction and improve air, water and nutrient movement. Thatch removal also permits better diffusion of air and moisture. Reducing compaction and thatch buildup results in a healthier, more vibrant lawn. Other advantages include enhanced soil oxygenation to support microbial activity, deeper root growth, and better fertilizer efficiency. Overseeding after aerating or dethatching takes advantage of the superior seed-to-soil contact.

Proper timing for core aeration and dethatching depends on the type of grass. For cool season turfs like fescue and bluegrass, early spring as soil temperatures climb above 55°F, allows aeration before the main flush of growth. Warm-season grasses like Bermuda can be aerated once they are actively growing in early to mid-summer. Early fall is ideal for cool-season grasses again, coupled with overseeding bare patches. Allow the lawn to rest for 4-5 days before and after aeration or dethatching to minimize disruption. Avoid aerating severely drought-stressed or waterlogged turf. Making at least 2-3 passes over the entire lawn provides uniform treatment. While temporarily damaging, the long-term payoff of annual core aeration and dethatching makes these tasks foundational for improved soil structure and healthier, better-rooted grass.

When shopping for aerators and power rakes, match the size of the machine to your lawn. Manual and walk-behind models work for lawns up to a quarter acre. Tractor-mounted or pull-behind units are needed for larger yards. Electric and gas-powered models reduce physical exertion. Look for tine depth adjustability and ease of changing tine spacing. Debris collection bags minimize cleanup. Durability and ease of maintenance are also important considerations when selecting equipment. Proper usage and timing of aeration, dethatching, and overseeding reduces soil compaction, lessens thatch, enhances nutrient and water absorption, deeper rooting, and thicker, greener grass.

When aerating, apply weight or allow the tines to self-penetrate. Don't force the tines in by applying downward pressure, as this compacts soil. Make repeated perpendicular passes for even plug removal across the entire lawn. For cool-season grasses, aerate in early fall when night temperatures drop to 55°F, but growth remains active. Let the plugs dry and crumble before mowing. Overseed or apply starter fertilizer after aeration. Avoid aerating drought-dormant grasses. For warm-season turf, aerate during peak summer growth once soils are moist again after heat dormancy. Always water deeply the day before aerating.

When dethatching, adjust the tine depth to remove matted layers but not dig into the soil. Make several passes in different directions for thorough thatch removal. For cool-season turfs, dethatch in early fall prior to overseeding bare spots. For bermudagrass, dethatch in late spring before summer growth takes off. Remove excessive debris to prevent smothering grass. Allow the lawn to dry before irrigation, mowing, and fertilization after dethatchingto avoid damage to tender new growth underneath. Let grass plants recover fully before any additional management practices. Perform core aeration and power raking when grass is actively growing to limit stress and accelerate recovery.

Proper lawn aeration and dethatching requires using the right equipment and techniques matched to your grass type and lawn size. While causing short-term damage, the long-term benefits to soil compaction, thatch reduction, deeper rooting, enhanced nutrient and water intake, and thicker turf make core-aerating and power-raking fundamental practices for a healthy, thriving lawn. Taking advantage of improved seed-to-soil contact after these tasks by overseeding maximizes the results. Although disruptive, committing to annual core aeration and dethatching will pay dividends through substantially improved soil quality and grass growth.

5.4 on Spreaders & Sprayers:

Applying fertilizers, seeds, and lawn chemicals relies on using equipment suited to your lawn size and terrain. Spreaders evenly distribute granular products across the turf while sprayers apply liquids like herbicides and foliar nutrients. Choosing a spreader or sprayer that matches your needs, ensures accurate, uniform coverage. Walk-behind rotary and drop spreaders work for small yards. Towed spreaders cover ground quicker. Sprayers range from hand-pumped to backpack and tow-behind power models. When selecting equipment, look for sturdy construction, calibration adjustability, and ease of maintenance. Proper calibration tailored to your products and rates prevents wasted chemicals and uneven results.

Rotary or centrifugal spreaders use a spinning disk to broadcast granules over a 3-40 foot swath, depending on model size. Benefits include fast coverage, simple controls, and resistance to clogging. Limitations include less precision around landscaping, the potential for uneven spreading, and fertilizer burn if overlaps lead to double application. Durable gears, reinforced catch hopper, enclosed disk drive, pneumatic tires, and adjustable deflectors control spread width. Corrosion-resistant poly hoppers and undercarriage scrapers to prevent buildup are useful features. Test for uniform pattern at different settings.

Drop or gravity spreaders meter granules directly below in 1-8 foot bands using a gate-type mechanism. They allow better control and precision around gardens. Limitations include slower application over large areas and potential for striping. Look for metal gears, smooth dispenser action, an edge guard to guidethe flow, and pneumatic tires. Close setting adjustments provide precision. Dual spinners permit splitting the flow for two passes at half rate, improving uniformity.

For large areas, tow-behind spreaders attach to tractors or ATVs, covering 30-40 feet. Benefits include fast coverage, large capacity, and attachment versatility, and the features are heavy-duty gears, clutch drive engagement, flow divider, generous hopper, calibration system, pneumatic tires, and adjustable deflectors. An apron front contains the throw, and it hasseek easy-to-access controls and a stable hitch.

Sprayers apply liquid products like herbicides, wetting agents, and foliar nutrients. Different types include hand pumped, backpack, tow-behind, and hose-end models. Powered sprayers work best for large areas. Sought after features include evaluated pump quality, tank capacity, wand comfort, nozzle versatility and filtration. Other useful features are pressure regulation, agitation, and easy tank cleaning. Consistent spray patterns and filtration prevent nozzle clogging.

Proper calibration tailored to your products and desired rates ensures accurate application. Check calibration regularly, as wear affects settings. First, determine the recommended rate from the label. Next, choose equipment settings based on manufacturer guidelines for that rate. Finally, test and refine with a measured trial area. Recheck calibrations periodically all season.

When using spreaders and sprayers, employ techniques for uniform coverage without waste, lawn damage, or runoff. Walk or drive at a steady pace in perpendicular passes. Avoid overlaps creating double application. Check the flow to prevent clogging. Use edge guards and deflectors properly, and clean after each use. Follow all label precautions for safe chemical handling.

Choosing rotary, drop, or tow-behind spreaders based on lawn size and terrain efficiently covers small yards to large acreages. Hand-pumped to powered sprayers suit small spot applications for entire lawn pesticide treatments. Taking time to properly calibrate equipment settings to your products and desired rates helps ensure accurate, uniform distribution every time. Careful operating practices prevent wasted products and lawn damage while protecting the surrounding environment. Properly matched, calibrated, and operated spreaders and sprayers are essential tools for effective lawn care.

When selecting a spreader, opt for a model matching your lawn's square footage and terrain. Handheld and walk-behind rotary or drop spreaders accommodate small, flat lawns up to a quarter acre. Tow-behind spreaders attach to ATVs or tractors to efficiently cover large, rolling expanses over an acre in size. Seek corrosion-resistant poly hoppers, sturdy gears, enclosed drives, and pneumatic tires for durability. Deflectors or edge guards control spread width and prevent throwing product where its not wanted. Calibration adjustments and coverage testing ensure even application rates tailored to your particular fertilizer.

For sprayers, hand-pumped backpack units suit small spot treatments. Tow-behind power sprayers work best for overall lawn application. Look for high-volume, high-pressure pumps and adequate tank capacity to minimize refilling. Wands should have comfortable grips and adjustable nozzles for varied spray patterns. Helpful features include agitators to prevent settling, pressure regulators for consistent flow, and filtration systems to reduce clogging. Easy-fill, drain and clean tanks quicken maintenance. Nozzle quality impacts distribution uniformity.

Consistent calibration is crucial for accurate coverage. Consult labels for product spreading/spraying rates. Adjust equipment settings based on manufacturer guidelines for achieving that rate. Perform test runs on measured areas and tweak settings to dial-in uniform distribution. Recheck calibrations over the season as wear alters application. Employing careful techniques prevents skips, overlaps, and waste. Always follow label safety precautions when using chemicals. Properly matching equipment type to lawn size, frequent calibrations and careful use ensures fertilizers and treatments are accurately applied for an effective lawn program. Correctly applying fertilizers, chemicals, and other lawn treatments relies on selecting, spreading, and spraying equipment tailored to your lawn size and terrain. Walk-behind rotary and drop spreader models work well for small, flat yards. Tow-behind spreaders attach to ATVs or tractors to efficiently cover large acreages. Hand-pumped backpack sprayers suit spot chemical treatments, while engine-driven tow-behind sprayers are better for overall lawn application.

When choosing spreaders, match capacity and features to lawn square footage. Handheld and smaller walk-behind spreaders accommodate up to 10,000 square feet. Larger tow-behind models can handle over an acre. Seek sturdy construction with corrosion-resistant poly hoppers, enclosed drives, robust gears, and pneumatic tires to withstand use on uneven ground. Deflectors or edge guards control spread width and prevent throwing products where not intended. Settings for adjusting spread width and rate should be easy to customize.

For sprayers, hand-pumped backpack units accommodate spot treatments. Tow-behind power sprayers work best for lawn chemical application. The key features are pump volume/pressure, tank capacity, wand comfort, agitators, and filtration. Nozzle quality and adjustments impact distribution uniformity. Look for easy filling, draining, and tank rinsing.

Consistent calibration tailored to your products and target application rates is crucial for accuracy. Consult labels for recommended spreading/spraying amounts per area. Adjust equipment settings based on manufacturer guidelines to achieve those amounts. Perform test runs on measured lawn sections, tweaking settings to dial-in uniform coverage. Recheck calibrations periodically as wear alters application over time.

When operating spreaders and sprayers, use good techniques for even, consistent coverage without waste, lawn damage or runoff. Walk/drive at a steady, measured pace in straight overlapping passes. Make a second set of perpendicular passes to ensure penetration into any tracks. Check flow and pattern consistency, watching for changes indicating obstructions. Avoid excessive overlaps leading to potential lawn burning from double doses. Use edge guards, deflectors, and shields properly to contain products only in target areas. Always follow label safety precautions when handling chemicals.

Properly matching spreader and sprayer types to lawn size, frequent calibrations tailored to products and target rates, and employing careful operating practices ensure fertilizers, pesticides, and other treatments cover turf uniformly without waste, skips, or environmental contamination. Selecting the right broadcast, drop, or tow-behind spreader model, and a hand-pumped or engine-driven sprayer based on lawn terrain and area provides an efficient toolset. Dialing in properly calibrated settings and exercising cautious distribution techniques result in more accurate, effective lawn treatment through optimal fertilizer and chemical coverage.

5.5 Hand Tools:

Basic hand tools are essential for performing many lawn care tasks. While power equipment like mowers and string trimmers handle the bulk of lawn maintenance, hand tools provide more control for detailed work. Choose quality tools suited to your needs and maintain them properly for years of use. This section covers common hand tool types, key features to look for, and proper use and care.

Lawn Rakes

Lawn rakes level an area in preparation for seeding or smoothing after aeration. Metal tine rakes remove debris without disturbing soil. Plastic tines are more flexible. A leveling or landscape rake has short, stiff tines ideal for smoothing. For fall leaf removal, a fan rake with a wide curved head quickly gathers leaves. Bow rakes have longer tines and cover more area.

Seeking smooth, straight tines mounted securely to a sturdy handle is important. Fiberglass and hardwood handles provide durability and shock absorption. Look for rakes sized appropriately for your hands with cushioned grips for comfort. Spring brake mechanisms allow flexing when encountering rocks and roots.

Hand Tillers

Hand tillers cultivate soil and mix amendments in vegetable gardens and flower beds. The claw-like tines stir the soi, while a serrated edge cuts roots and sod. Loop-style tillers ease digging with less strain. Seek sturdy metal construction. Ergonomic handles should fit your grip and swing comfortably.

Loppers

Loppers prune overgrown lawn edges and cut through small branches and saplings up to 2 inches thick. Compound action models multiply leverage with pivot arms. Anvil types have a blade cutting against a flat surface. Bypass loppers use two curved blades like scissors.

Look for carbon steel blades that resist dulling. Low-friction pivot points make cutting easier. Handles should be cushioned grip and sized for your hand. Avoid heavy loppers that fatigue your hands and arms quickly during prolonged use.

Pruners

Pruners trim errant tree suckers, woody weeds, and damaged lawn edges. Bypass pruners have two curved blades passing each other like scissors for clean cuts. Anvil types have a straight blade cutting against a flat surface, pinching material first.

Quality pruners have tempered steel blades that hold an edge. A tension adjuster provides proper blade alignment over time. Ergonomic grip handles reduce hand strain. Look for a rotating handle knob to adjust orientation. A sap groove on the blade prevents sticking. Hand size and cutting tasks determine length.

Hoes

Hoes disrupt soil crusts, remove weeds, and create planting rows in vegetable gardens. A Dutch hoe has a broad blade angled to skim just below the surface. Scuffle hoes have an oscillating blade scraping the top inch. Warren hoes create narrow furrows with two angled blades.

Seek solid blade-to-handle joints and cushioned grips. Forward-angled blades work best for hoeing weeds, while square blades are for trenching and furrowing. Match blade width to rows. Narrow blades provide more precision.

Trowels

Garden trowels dig holes for bulbs and small plants. Heavy-duty transplanting trowels feature thicker steel and handle protection. The contoured blade scoops and lifts soil easily. Ergonomic handles provide leverage and reduce hand strain.

Look for one-piece steel blade-to-handle construction. Stainless steel offers lasting rust resistance but less soil penetration. A cushioned grip provides comfort, while wider handles improve torque. Select a scoop width suited to typical planting tasks.

Cultivators

Cultivators and hand weeders uproot weeds and break up surface crusting. Serrated edges or curved prongs work around established plants without damage. A long-handled cultivator extends reach to hand weed large areas comfortably.

Durable steel with fiberglass handles provides strength and reduced fatigue. Ash hardwood handles also work well. Look for a cushioned grip and prongs spaced approximately 1 to 1.5 inches apart. The handle angle lets you apply downward pressure while digging in. While power equipment handles the bulk of lawn maintenance, hand tools provide more control for detailed work. Investing in quality tools matched to your needs and properly caring for them ensures lasting performance. Essential hand tools include rakes, hoes, pruners, loppers, trowels, and cultivators.

When selecting hand tools, prioritize durable steel construction with secure blade-to-handle joints. Fiberglass and hardwood handles absorb shock and cushion hands. Size the tools appropriately for your hands and typical tasks. Maintain sharp cutting edges and proper adjustment. Clean tools after use and store them securely.

Quality rakes have tines firmly mounted to sturdy handles. Metal fan rakes quickly gather leaves. Stiff, short-tined landscape rakes smooth lawns. Cushioned grips provide comfort. Spring brakes prevent snapping if hitting rocks. Hoes should have sturdy blade-to-handle joints and blades matched to weeding or trenching tasks. Cushioned grips reduce hand fatigue.

Top pruners and loppers have tempered steel blades that hold an edge. Low-friction pivots ease cutting smoothness. Sap grooves prevent sticking. Cushioned, ergonomic handles minimize strain. Hand size and cutting tasks determine the appropriate length. Keep blades sharpened for easiest cutting.

Look for trowels with one-piece steel construction and cushioned grip. Match trowel scoop width to common planting jobs. Space cultivator prongs 1-1.5 inches apart to easily penetrate soil around established plants. Long-handled models expand reach.

Maintain hand tools by regularly sharpening cutting edges, lubricating pivots, checking handles for secure fastening, and touching up nicks in metal parts to prevent rust. Clean off debris after each use. Avoid leaving tools exposed to outdoor elements.

When using hand tools, wear protective gloves and safety glasses. Select ergonomic tools sized for your hands to prevent muscle strains. Take breaks to stretch and change hand positions. Use the right tool for each task and avoid improper substitutions that can cause injury. For example, don't use a shovel to pry roots.

Invest in essential hand tools suited to your needs. Keep blades sharpened and handles secure, and properly care for them to ensure the right implements are always ready for lawn and garden work. Using properly sized ergonomic tools and protective gear keeps hand tool use safe and effective.

Rakes should have tines sized appropriately for leaves or smoothing soil and securely joined to handles. Grip material matters less than the proper handle angle and length for your height. Storage racks keep rakes accessible yet protected.

Hoe blades angled for weeding maximize efficiency over row crop styles requiring stooping. Oscillating edges avoid dulling like solid blades. Conserve effort with razor blades easily replaced when worn. Ergonomic handles reduce repetitive motion injuries.

Forged alloy steel pruner blades retain sharpness. Low-friction coatings on pivoting parts minimize required pressure. Sap grooves limit sticking. Rotating handles and grip size modifications accommodate different hand shapes. Clean blades with a disinfectant.

While power cultivators till entire plots, hand tools loosen soil precisely. Interchangeable heads provide the right till shape each season. Counterbalanced handles offset weight yet resist flexing. Use sandpaper and files to expose fresh edges on worn tines.

Hand tools last generations if properly maintained. True blades with sharpening stones. Sand then oil wooden handles splitting from weathering. Use touch-up paint on any unvarnished metal. Lubricate hinges and swivels to prevent rust. A clean, dry storage area protects investments.

The appropriate hand tool reduces strain and prevents injury. Well-maintained implements work better and safer. Taking breaks, hydrating sufficiently, and using both hands evenly distribute effort. Pay attention to hazards like underground pipes or powerlines. Investing in quality hand tools and properly caring for them delivers lasting returns through safer, easier lawn care.

5.6 Safety Equipment:

Lawn care involves using potentially dangerous equipment and chemicals. Making safety a priority requires employing proper protective gear and handling practices. This section covers essential safety equipment, when to use different items, and how to work as safely as possible when caring for your lawn.

Safety Glasses & Goggles

Eye protection guards against flying debris when mowing, using string trimmers, aerating, and performing other tasks. Traditional shielded safety glasses provide basic impact protection. Goggles form a protective seal around the eyes, preventing entry of dust and chemicals.

Select safety eyewear rated for high-velocity impacts. Lenses should be scratch-resistant. Opt for fog-resistant models that maintain clarity. Look for ventilation to reduce moisture buildup. Straps should allow a secure fit. Consider prescription safety glasses customized to your vision needs.

Face Shields

Face shields provide full front-of-face protection when using brush cutters, chainsaws, and other equipment. Visors extend fromthe forehead to below the chin. Mesh masks shield against debris while improving ventilation. Some shields attach to hard hats or safety glasses.

Seeks sturdy polycarbonate material that is heat, impact, and shatter resistant. Fog-free coatings maintain visibility. The headgear should adjust for a secure fit and comfort. Look for padded forehead rests on models worn directly. Consider hearing protection earmuffs for noisy equipment.

Protective Gloves

Gloves safeguard hands from blisters, cuts, and abrasions when using tools and handling soil, fertilizer, and chemicals. Leather, canvas, and suede gloves resist punctures. Rubber gloves protect against chemicals. Cotton provides ventilation when pulling weeds.

Match glove material and thickness to the task. A tight fit at the fingers and wrist prevents dragging. Opt for longer cuffs or gauntlets covering the forearms when handling irritants. Machine washable cotton makes cleaning easy. Replace any gloves showing wear or tears.

Foot Protection

Sturdy boots or shoes protect feet from falling tools, mower blades, and chemicals. Thick soles cushion against sharp objects. Steel or ceramic toe caps guard against crushing injuries. Waterproof materials like rubber boots resist chemicals.

Look for slip-resistant soles to prevent falls on slick grass. Ankle support provides stability on uneven terrain. Mesh panels or side vents keep feet cool. Consider attaching puncture-proof foot guards for string trimmers and brush cutters. Replace worn or damaged boots promptly.

Hearing Protection

Power equipment like mowers, blowers, and brushcutters generate dangerous noise levels. Foam earplugs or earmuffs buffer sound waves to protect hearing. Earmuffs surround the entire ear. Some models cancel noise while amplifying voices.

Seek comfort and appropriate noise reduction ratings (NRR) for your equipment. A variety of sizes and materials, like silicone, allow for a customized fit. Look for breathable models that prevent moisture buildup during extended wear. Keep multiple ear protectors handy for others.

Respiratory Protection

Dust masks filter out grass clippings, pollen, and chemicals when mowing or applying treatments. Disposable paper masks work for short durations. Reusable respirators with filter cartridges protect longer against vapors or fine particles.

Select close-fitting masks rated for lawn chemical exposures. Straps must provide a secure seal. Choose filters suited for particulates, gases, or dual combinations. Look for vented models that reduce heat buildup. Keep extra filters on hand. Replace disposable masks regularly. Caring for a lawn involves the frequent use of potentially dangerous equipment and chemicals, making safety a crucial priority. Employing proper protective gear matched to the task and cautious equipment handling and work practices reduces preventable injury risk.

Eye protection like impact-resistant safety glasses or goggles guards against flying debris when mowing, trimming, and performing repairs. Face shields provide full front-of-face protection when using brush cutters, chainsaws, and similar equipment. Look for sturdy, puncture-resistant gloves suited to each task, whether heavy leather for equipment use or breathable cotton for pulling weeds. Respirators and dust masks filter out grass clippings, chemical particulates, and vapors encountered during lawn maintenance. Selecting earplugs and earmuffs to match noise reduction needs protects hearing from hazardous equipment levels.

Choose safety eyewear that fits securely and maintain clear lenses for optimum visibility. Take advantage of prescription safety glasses customized to your vision needs. Ensure face shields provide adjustable, stable headgear for full face coverage. With gloves, focus on fit, coverage, and durability for the task. Keep multiple disposable dust masks on hand for others. Confirm respirators seal properly and change filter cartridges regularly.

Look for moisture-wicking, breathable materials when selecting protective gear used for extended periods to avoid discomfort. Take time to put on all appropriate safety equipment before each task.

Beyond personal protective equipment, establishing proper practices is crucial:
Read all manuals thoroughly.
Clear work areas of hazards.
Maintain a safe stance and control when operating equipment.
Shut down and check for damage if striking objects.
Avoid rushing or distractions.

Making lawn care safety the priority, not an afterthought, reduces preventable injury risks significantly. Invest in quality protective gear matched to tasks, check it regularly for deterioration, replace worn items promptly, and use all appropriate equipment for the job. Combining protective gear with proper safe handling practices ensures the safest environment when caring for your lawn.

Jamie Tukey

Chapter 6
Lawn Alternatives

6.1 - Groundcovers

For homeowners looking to reduce or eliminate grass on their property, groundcovers offer an attractive, low-maintenance alternative. From spreading perennials to dense, mat-forming plants, groundcovers are useful for controlling erosion, suppressing weeds, and replacing labor-intensive lawns. When selected and cared for properly, groundcovers create beautiful, lush carpets of color and texture.

When choosing a groundcover, it's important to consider your climate and growing conditions. Look for plants suitable for your hardiness zone that match the site's sunlight, soil type, and moisture levels. Factor in mature size, growth rate, and spreading tendency to avoid future maintenance headaches. Groundcovers that spread aggressively by runners or rhizomes require more diligent pruning to keep them in bounds. Slower-growing varieties like sedums may take longer to establish but don't need frequent reining in.

It's also wise to decide whether you want a single-species groundcover or a diverse mix of plants. Monocultures offer uniformity but are more vulnerable to pest and disease problems. Incorporating a variety of groundcovers increases visual interest, provides multiple seasons of color, and helps strengthen the plant community against environmental stresses. Combining spreading groundcovers with low-growing perennials, ornamental grasses, bulbs, and annuals is a practical polyculture approach.

Proper preparation is crucial when installing groundcovers. Eliminate existing vegetation, digging out any invasive weeds and grasses. For large areas, smothering with UV-stabilized tarps or repeated glyphosate applications may be necessary. When soil is bare, improve drainage and incorporate organic matter like compost. Realize that groundcovers often take 2-3 years to fully establish, so patience and persistence are vital.

Plant spacing depends on the mature size of your chosen groundcovers. Low, dense growers like Ajuga can be planted 4-6 inches apart. More vigorous spreaders like English ivy and Vinca minor need 12-18 inches between plants. Containerized stock is recommended over seeds, cuttings, or plugs to provide immediate covering. Water new plantings daily until their root systems develop. A layer of mulch helps retain moisture and suppress weeds during establishment.

Ongoing care also ensures healthy, attractive groundcover areas. Apply fertilizer and organic matter in early spring and fall. Prune over-exuberant growers as needed to prevent encroachment. Weed regularly when plants are young and vulnerable. Irrigate during droughts but avoid excessive moisture that encourages diseases. Some evergreen groundcovers may require winter protection in colder climates. With proper selection, preparation, and maintenance, groundcovers provide a colorful, carefree alternative to traditional turfgrass lawns. When selecting groundcovers, you have many attractive options to consider for your landscape. Some top choices include:

Creeping Phlox - A classic spring bloomer, CreepingPphlox produces carpets of colorful flowers in shades of pink, purple, blue, and white. Cultivars offer variations in bloom time, flower color, and growth habits. This sturdy perennial grows 4-6 inches tall and spreads 12 inches per year. It thrives in full sun or light shade with well-drained soil.

English Ivy - For shade gardens, English ivy is a popular groundcover choice. Its glossy lobed leaves remain green throughout winter, providing year-round cover. Climbing stems attach to surfaces, while horizontal stems creep along the ground. Left unpruned, ivy can become invasive, so containment is required.

Japanese Pachysandra - With its broad green leaves, pachysandra forms a lush, uniform carpet in shady areas. Tiny white flowers bloom in spring but aren't very showy. Grow 6-12 inches tall and space plants 8-12 inches apart for quick coverage. Takes well to shearing.

Creeping Juniper - An evergreen needle-leaved groundcover, creeping juniper handles heat, wind, and drought once established. Varieties range from prostrate forms 1-2 feet tall to more upright types reaching 6 feet. Rugged and low-maintenance but spreads slowly.

Sweet Woodruff - A favorite for shade gardens, sweet woodruff has fragrant, star-shaped white flowers in spring. Its whorls of lance-shaped leaves remain green or turn red-bronze in winter. Grows 6-8 inches tall and spreads quickly via underground runners. Combines well with spring bulbs.

Blue Star Creeper - For rock gardens or between stepping stones, blue star creeper provides a dense mat of foliage covered in starry, light blue flowers in spring. Grows only 2-4 inches tall but spreads rapidly across sunny, well-drained sites. Shear back spent blooms to encourage reblooming.

Wooly Thyme - Soft gray-green leaves make wooly thyme a living carpet for hot, sunny areas with poor soil. Pink or white blooms appear in early summer. Combines nicely with other low-growing perennials, grasses, and bulbs. Stays under 3 inches tall and spreads slowly. Withstands light foot traffic.

Snow-In-Summer - Charming white fuzz on succulent leaves makes this aptly named for rock gardens and borders. Heat and drought tolerant once established. Grows 4-6 inches tall and spreads moderately. Pink flowers contrast nicely with foliage in early summer. Mix with bulbs or spring annuals.

Periwinkle - Two popular, fast-spreading options are greater periwinkle (Vinca major) for shade and common periwinkle (Vinca minor) for sun. If pruned back, both have glossy evergreen leaves and bright blue blooms from spring to early summer. Can be invasive, so contain or use sterile varieties.

Wintercreeper - An adaptable evergreen groundcover for sun or shade. Small glossy leaves turn purplish in fall and winter. Inconspicuous flowers in spring. Varied growth habits from 6 inches to 3 feet tall, so choose carefully. Responds well to pruning.

Carex - With over 100 species, this sedge family offers many great groundcover choices like C. buchananii or C. oshimensis. Evergreen grassy leaves form low mounds or spreading patches. Deer resistant and drought tolerant once established. Combines well with stepping stones or as a lawn alternative.

The possibilities are endless for replacing turf or blank mulch with beautiful, easy-care groundcovers. Take time to assess your site's growing conditions, space constraints, and aesthetic preferences to pick the perfect plant. With the right selection and care, you'll be rewarded with an enviable carpet of color.

6.2 - Rock Gardens

For a unique, low-maintenance alternative to lawn, consider installing an ornamental rock garden. Also called alpine or scree gardens, these displays allow you to creatively combine rocks, gravel, and carefully selected plants. Rocky outcrops bring visual interest and textural contrast to the landscape while providing an ideal growing environment for drought-tolerant, sun-loving species. With proper design and upkeep, rock gardens offer years of durable, natural beauty.

Choosing a Site

The ideal rock garden location receives full sun for at least six hours daily. This ensures good flowering and helps heat-loving plants thrive. While drainage is key, don't situate the garden in an area prone to excessive drought. Consider existing topography and aim for a slight slope to encourage drainage. Incorporate any natural rock outcrops or boulders already present on the site. Locate your garden near paths or sitting areas so it can be easily viewed and maintained.

Building Up Base Layers

Constructing the garden atop a gravel sub-base improves drainage while allowing you to contour the bed's shape. Use coarse stone like half-inch drainage rock or pea gravel as your bottom layer, 4-6 inches deep. Over this, add 2-4 inches of finer gravel, such as pea gravel, or decomposed granite to form the surface layer. Mounded earth underneath gives you greater flexibility for sculpting elevation changes.

Incorporating Hardscape

Artfully arrange attractive rocks and boulders on top of the gravel base. Opt for a mix of stone sizes, colors, and shapes for visual diversity. Locallyl quarried rock matches your regional geology, but consider importing types like granite, sandstone, or limestone for distinct appearances. Stack flat-sided rocks to build ledges, use rounded river rock in stream beds, or inset large statement boulders as focal points.

Plant Selection Basics

When choosing rock garden plants, seek out alpines and perennials suited to fast drainage, heat reflection, and lean soil. Evergreens like sedums, rock cress, and creeping phlox provide year-round color and structure. Small bulbs like squill, grape hyacinth, and crocus thrive nestled in rocky crevices. For summer blooms, opt for low-growing species with brightly-colored flowers. Utilize native plants adapted to your climate and growing conditions for easy success.

Allow enough space between plants to account for spreading. Mass groupings of 3-5 plants together for impact. Use dwarf conifers, ornamental grasses, or trailing succulents to add height and volume. Consider annuals for quick color in first-year gardens before perennials fill in. Aim for diversity in plant textures, forms and flowering seasons for long-lasting interest. When establishing plants, amend the gravel base layers with organic matter like compost or aged manure to enrich the soil. Water new plantings thoroughly and as needed until established. Beyond watering, maintenance needs are low. Prune back leggy growth in spring to encourage compact form. Shelter alpines from winter wet and cold in harsh climates. Weed carefully by hand around delicate root systems. Fertilize sparingly, if at all, to avoid excessive growth. Monitor for pests like spider mites or scale that can thrive in hot, dry conditions.

Every few years, cut back overgrown plants severly to rejuvenate them. Alternatively, divide congested clumps in early spring or fall. Replant divisions elsewhere or share with gardening friends. Over time, refurbish mulch between plants to suppress weeds and retain moisture. Top off gravel if it migrates downward into soil layers. Incorporate fresh rocks periodically for renewed interest and artistry.

Some great plants for rock gardens include low-growing sedums, dianthus, euphorbias, and creeping thymes that thrive in hot, dry ,and poor soil. Alpine varieties of penstemon, lewisia, and rock cress add vertical elements, and bright bursts of spring and summer blooms. Mat-forming hens and chicks and evergreen succulents like sedums provide year-round structure and color. Small bulbs like crocus, grape hyacinth, and squill flourish nestled among artfully arranged rocks and boulders.

With a thoughtful layout utilizing full sun and excellent drainage, proper plant choices, and attentive care, rock gardens offer a stunning alternative to traditional lawns or foundation plantings. The intricate artistry and seasonal interest are well worth the initial effort. Sedums come in upright and creeping varieties like Autumn Joy, Dragon's Blood, and Angelina that offer colorful evergreen foliage and late summer blooms. Hens and chicks form mats of symmetrical rosettes ranging from 2-12 inches wide in green, gray, or red-tinged options. Fragrant, spreading thymes, like creeping thyme, form carpets of foliage topped with purple or pink flowers in summer. They need good drainage. Compact perennial dianthus features blue-gray leaves and colorful single or double blooms in summer. Include alpine types well-suited to rock gardens.

Euphorbias, like cushion spurge and myrsinites, have chartreuse flowers and thrive in poor, dry soil, and full sun. Lewisia is a native succulent that blooms with satiny flowers in white, pink, orange, or yellow mid-spring into summer. Beardtongue penstemon adds vertical accents with tubular flowers in vibrant shades. Many penstemon varieties are drought-tolerant. Foam flower tiarella with short spikes of starry white flowers and heart-shaped leaves does well in shade and tolerates some moisture. Mat-forming evergreen perennials like aubrieta and alyssum rock cress contribute white or purple blooms in spring.

6.3 - Mulch Beds

For an easy, low-maintenance alternative to turfgrass, consider installing mulch beds around trees, foundations, and borders. Mulch beds utilize organic materials like wood chips, bark, leaves, or straw to form an attractive, weed-suppressing groundcover. Well-executed mulch beds prevent soil erosion, retain moisture, and add aesthetic interest to the landscape. With proper installation and refreshing, mulched areas provide a lush, finished look with minimal upkeep required.

Choosing Materials

Popular organic mulch options include shredded hardwood, softwood or cypress bark, wood chips, pine straw, shredded leaves, compost, peat moss, and cocoa hulls. Inorganic materials like pebbles, gravel, and recycled rubber are also available. Select a mulch that complements your plantings and home style. Deep earthy colors like brown work well among shrubs and trees, while bright red cedar complements contemporary designs. Attractive neutrals include blonde woods or black lava rock.

Consider decomposition rate, cost, texture, moisture retention, and replenishment needs when choosing materials. Long-lasting mulches, like pine bark, require less frequent replenishment than fast decomposing options like wood chips. Bulk purchases often save money. Fine, fluffy texture is suitable for formal beds while nuggets and chips work for rustic gardens. Test drainage and moisture before applying mulch around moisture-sensitive plants.

Site Preparation

Proper soil preparation is key to successful mulching. Remove all weeds before applying mulch, which can propagate weeds when directly placed on top. Aerate compacted soil and amend it with compost to improve fertility and drainage. Top-dress any low spots to create a level surface. You can apply mulch directly atop soil or first-line beds with newspapers or landscape fabric to optimize weed suppression. Outline mulch beds with edging to keep materials contained.

Installing Mulch

Apply 2-4 inches of mulch across prepared beds, keeping it an inch or two away from plant crowns. Shredded bark will knit together well, while wood chips may shift more over time. Rake mulch smooth across the area, feathering edges to create a seamless transition. Mulch depth will reduce through decomposition, so replenish annually to maintain effectiveness. Mulch develops a fine, aged look over time. Mimic this on new installs by scuffing up the surface after mulching.

Around trees, piling deep mulch against the trunk can cause moisture buildup and rotting. Maintain a buffer zone a few inches wide around the trunk, clear of mulch contact. Rake and refresh this ring yearly when replenishing overall mulch depth. Likewise, avoid mounding mulch against foundations or siding. Adequate airflow is vital. Replenish mulch annually in spring, or whenever it becomes thin. Rake old mulch to refresh the surface, and top it with fresh mulch up to the desired depth.. More frequent replenishment is needed for fast-decomposing mulches in rainy climates. Reapply only 1-2 inches per year to maintain proper soil oxygenation and airflow.

Monitor mulch beds regularly for weeds. Hand pull emerging weeds while small to prevent establishment. Spot treat persistent weeds with vinegar, borax, or corn gluten organic herbicides. Avoid using wood chips from diseased trees which may spread issues. Diseased mulch can be safely composted before use.

Annually, check for rodent tunnels or insect infestations in mulch, which can damage plant roots. Rake mulch flat to remove nesting spaces and tunnels. Report termite activity to a pest control professional. Wood mulches rarely deplete soil nitrogen but may require occasional fertilizer for optimal plant growth. Test the soil to determine its needs.

On slopes, use erosion control blankets under mulch to prevent displacement. Contain mulch beds on inclines with gravel borders or cut edging. Rain and gravity displace mulch over time. Replenish low spots and return stray mulch to beds to maintain coverage. A disciplined yearly renewal regimen prevents major mulch migration issues.

If remodeling a bed's shape or plant composition, completely remove the old mulch before reinstalling fresh mulch. Rototilling or removal by wheelbarrow allows redesigning and soil amending as needed. Mulch installation requires some periodic labor but saves more time compared to lawn mowing, edging, and weeding. Well-maintained mulch beds provide a polished yet low-maintenance look.

Creative Touches

Beyond covering basic planting beds, mulch can be used decoratively to enhance landscapes. Frame drainage swales, paths, and patios with a fresh border of contrasting mulch. Accent boulders, features, or specimen plants by mounding deep mulch in rings around their bases. Establish new planting pockets within turf using mulch "islands." Edge vegetable gardens or herb beds with mulch walkways.

Shape mulch into creative patterns like sweeping waves or outline embedded designs. Use colorful mulches like red lava rock or gold pine straw for eye-catching but natural accents. Coordinate mulch colors with flowering perennials, shrub foliage, and hardscape materials. Whether used simply or artfully, mulch beds offer an organic alternative for reducing lawn maintenance. Renewed annually, they deliver beautiful, finished effects with minimal demands on time or labor.

6.4 - Vegetable Gardens

For homeowners interested in gardening for food production, installing designated vegetable garden beds can be a rewarding alternative to traditional lawn spaces. Tailored vegetable gardens allow for intensive cultivation of food crops within a defined area while keeping the rest of the yard free for ornamental lawn uses. With proper planning and care, in-ground vegetable gardens can yield plentiful harvests of garden-fresh produce right at home.

Choosing a Site

When selecting a vegetable garden location, aim for a sunny, flat spot with at least 6 hours of direct sunlight daily. Well-draining, nutrient-rich soil with a pH between 6-7 is ideal but can be amended as needed. Avoid low areas prone to flooding or standing water. Consider proximity to water and compost sources for ease of maintenance. Locate gardens away from trees and shrubs to reduce root competition and shade issues.

For convenience, establish vegetable gardens close to your home and kitchen for easy access when harvesting and watering. However, ensure the placement allows enough pathway space around beds for movement and maintenance. Selecting a site near existing or planned hardscape features like fences, trellises, and sheds can take advantage of vertical growing space.

Garden Design Elements

Think about layout and dimensions to maximize planting capacity. Rectangular or square designs utilize space most efficiently. Incorporate wide aisles between raised beds to allow passing with a wheelbarrow. Orient rows running north to south to distribute sunlight evenly. Size gardens appropriately for your family's needs, from just a few beds to expansive multi-plot landscapes.

Include vertical structures like trellises and cages to support vining crops and optimize production. Use fencing or edging to deter animal pests from entering beds. Strategically placed arbors, pergolas, and plant screens can provide shade for heat-sensitive plants. Decorate plots with pathways, benches, art, and other personal touches to create an inviting garden space.

Soil Preparation

Prepare garden beds properly before planting. Test soil to determine needed amendments and pH adjustments. Till in several inches of organic compost to build fertility, drainage, and moisture retention. Level any uneven areas and clear roots, rocks, and debris. Rake smooth to form a fine planting bed. Or, build raised beds with imported planting mix to gain control over soil quality.

Consider installing drip irrigation, especially for arid climates. Prevent soilborne disease issues by rotating annual plant families each year across beds. Allow 3-4 years before replanting crops like tomatoes, peppers, or squash in the same spot. With mindful site selection, design, and soil preparation, you can establish a productive vegetable garden tailored to your gardening style and space constraints. Proper, ongoing care ensures a productive vegetable garden. Water deeply and consistently, about 1-2 inches per week, depending on climate. Applying mulch around plants retains moisture and reduces weeds. Determine fertilizer needs with soil tests and apply organic options like compost, manure, or fish emulsions. Stake and prune plants as needed for support and air circulation.

Monitor for insect pests and disease issues. Row covers and companion planting help protect crops. Remove and destroy severely infested plants and use organic sprays as a last resort. Weed weekly to prevent competition, especially when plants are young and vulnerable. Check ripening produce frequently for peak flavor at harvest.

As summer plants fade in fall, clear spent debris and add it to the compost pile. Planting cool-weather crops like kale, carrots, and lettuce extends the growing season into winter in milder climates. Leaving roots intact preserves nutrients; otherwise, work compost into empty beds.

To enrich the soil for spring:
Grow cover crops like clover, rye, and legumes, which can be tilled under before planting.
Rotate annual plant families across beds each season to disrupt disease cycles.
Consider taking some of the garden "offline" to rejuvenate soil fertility.

Creative Elements

Beyond basic growing space, consider fun touches to personalize your garden. Use arbors, trellises, cages, and raised beds for vertical interest. Include benches, stepping stones, ornaments, and art for whimsical accents. Plant attractive edible flowers like nasturtium and calendula, which draw pollinators. Allow select ornamentals like marigolds and flowering herbs to intermingle with edibles. Train vining crops onto decorative obelisks and supports.

For convenience, cluster salad greens, herbs, and other oft-picked crops together in easily accessible beds near walkways. Locate tidier plants like peppers and broccoli on garden edges as a visual border, and espalier fruit trees along fences or walls for space efficiency. Support Vyng upward with strings, hoops, or meshes to expand the planting area. With planning and creativity, a vegetable garden can be productive and personal, yielding wholesome food and an inviting oasis to relax in and savor nature's bounty.

6.5-FlowerGardens

For homeowners who enjoy gardening and cultivating colorful blooms, dedicating designated flower garden spaces can provide an appealing alternative to lawn turf. Tailored flower beds and borders allow for intensive planting and care of ornamental flowers and foliage within defined areas, keeping remaining lawn needs simplified. With proper planning and maintenance, flower gardens offer diverse visual interests and habitat benefits beyond a blank green sward.

Garden Types

Popular flower garden styles include focused cutting gardens to harvest for arrangements, island beds surrounded by lawns, meandering borders along hardscape edges, and focal point plantings accenting structures like fountains or art. Cottage-style gardens have an informal, rambling layout with self-sowing annuals and perennials. Knot gardens utilize geometric shapes and patterns for formality. Rock and alpine gardens feature delicate rock-loving species.

Garden Size and Layout

Consider existing structures, traffic patterns, and viewing perspectives when situating flower gardens. Locate them near outdoor living spaces where they can be regularly enjoyed. Scale the garden size appropriately for your level of commitment to ongoing upkeep. Casual perennial beds typically require less care than refined hybrid planting designs. Incorporate functional paths and workspaces for access during maintenance. Site gardens where they receive sufficient sunlight for the chosen plants to thrive.

Shapethe beds and borders to complement your home's architecture and style. Formal, elegant designs with boxwood hedging and parterres suit classical homes, while free-flowing beds with grasses and wildflowers fit craftsman bungalows. Curving lines and pathways create visual movement, while straight lines and grid layouts convey formality. Size paths adequately for garden access and tasks.

Soil Preparation

Thoroughly prepare garden beds by removing weeds, turfgrass, roots, and debris. Loosen and enrich the soil with several inches of organic compost worked deeply into the top layers. Improve drainage in heavy clay soils by incorporating compost, gypsum, or pine fines. Test pH and amend the soil as needed to support chosen plants. Investing time in proper soil preparation prevents future issues and nurtures healthy root growth.

With mindful site selection, layout, design style, and soil enrichment, you can craft flower gardens that productively replace lawn while adding beauty, habitat, cut flowers, and visual organization to your landscape.Choose plants suited to your climate, site conditions, and design style. Select a variety of heights, forms, colors and bloom seasons for year-round interest. Mix sun-lovers and shade-tolerant plants in suitable microclimates within beds. Include pollinator-friendly native species along with ornamental specimens. Place larger, anchor plants first, then fill in with shorter flowers and foliage. Allow enough spacing for plants to reach mature sizes.

Ongoing Care

Cultivate consistently around plants, avoiding root damage. Mulch beds to conserve moisture and reduce weeds. Water thoroughly during droughts, aiming for 1-2 inches per week, depending on the climate. Stake and prune plants as needed. Remove spent flowers and foliar to tidy beds. Shear back leggy perennials in spring to encourage full, compact growth.

Test soil yearly and amend organically with compost as needed to nurture fertility. Watch for pest and disease issues and address them with integrated organic methods. Weed vigilantly when plants are young and vulnerable. As plants mature, they will fill in to outcompete weeds. In fall, leave healthy perennials standing for winter interest and seed distribution. Once frost blackens foliage, cut back and add clippings to compost piles.

Over time, divide overgrown clumps to rejuvenate plants. Redesign and edit bed layouts periodically to refresh appearances as gardens evolve. Allowing some self-sowing creates a casual charm, but monitor seedling spread to avoid unwanted takeovers. With attentive care and well-chosen plant diversity tailored to your site and preferences, ornamental flower gardens provide vibrant living alternatives to turfgrass lawns.

Creative Touches

Look for ways to impart personality and whimsy in your flower gardens. Include benches, trellises, stepping stones, and garden art. Train vines onto obelisks and fences for vertical interest. Mulch paths in a contrasting colosr and textures to define garden spaces. Allow select edibles like herbs and nasturtiums to intermingle with flowers. Site specimen trees, containers, and statuary as focal points at axis intersections and bed corners. Include year-round structure with grasses, seed heads, and evergreen foliage and shrubs. With planning and creativity, flower gardens offer far more than well-tended beauty – they become outdoor living spaces in which to enjoy and find daily inspiration in.

6.6 - Hardscapes

Incorporating decorative hardscapes provides an appealing alternative for homcowncrs sccking to rcducc high-maintcnancc lawn arcas. Hardscapes like patios, pathways, decks, and driveways effectively limit or replace turfgrass while adding visual interest, functionality, and organization to the landscape. With a thoughtful design approach and proper installation, hardscaping delivers durable, low-care solutions for converting lawn spaces into inviting outdoor living areas.

Beyond reducing mowing and maintenance demands, thoughtfully designed hardscapes offer many benefits. They provide added living space for cooking, dining, entertaining, play, and relaxation. Pathways extended through and around planted beds allow greater access and outdoor enjoyment. Raised planters and beds enable accessible gardening without ground-level kneeling. Hardscapes can enhance curb appeal and architectural style with coordinated designs and materials. Functional spaces for vehicle parking and equipment storage help organize landscape uses. Properly graded surfaces direct site drainage as part of an overall stormwater control plan. Hardscape steps, ramps, and pathways improve safety and accessibility around the home. Vertical gardening opportunities exist with trellises, walls, and fences incorporated into the design.

Quality hardscape materials should suit the climate, design style, and budget for long-lasting beauty and durability. Concrete offers versatility and economy but requires sealing maintenance. Stamped patterns, stains, and mosaic inlays can add decorative flair. Brick has a classic look well-suited for patios and walkways, with permeable versions aiding drainage. Flagstone provides a natural appearance that works well in informal, eclectic designs. Tile delivers diverse shapes, colors, and textures, though it performs best in warmer, milder climates. Gravel offers a simple, organic look and feel but requires edging containment and a potential weed barrier. Wood is an affordable decking option if pressure-treated correctly, though it requires regular sealing and is not ideal for walks or drives. Proper planning, material selection, base preparation, and installation techniques ensure your hardscaping investment realizes its full aesthetic and functional potential while reducing lawn maintenance obligations. Carefully think through how you want to use and enjoy new hardscape spaces. Gather inspiration from books, websites, and public gardens. Sketch layout ideas to conceptualize plans. Consider existing architecture, traffic flows, views, sunlight patterns, and drainage factors. Decide on a style from sleek modern to classic brick walkways to harmonize with your home.

Determine how hardscapes will integrate and transition into adjacent lawn areas and planted beds. Include cohesive design details like matching edging materials. Account for future plant growth to avoid engulfment. Locate hardscapes advantageously to limit leftover fragmented turf patches that are awkward to mow around.

For best results, hire a professional landscape designer to translate your vision into a master plan, addressing style cohesion, spatial flow, and construction feasibility. Ensure your landscape contractor thoroughly reviews plans and communicates any installation concerns beforehand. Phase projects gradually to spread costs over time as the budget allows.

Ongoing Care

Allow freshly installed hardscapes to cure completely before use; up to 28 days for concrete. Remove construction debris and backfill gap edges with matching material to finish spaces. Yearly maintenance involves cleaning accumulated debris with a broom or pressure washer. Reseal surfaced areas as needed, following manufacturer guidelines.

Watch for erosion, soil settling, and freeze-thaw cracks over time. Repair minor cracks with patching products and re-sand joints between pavers as needed. Address drainage issues immediately to prevent expensive problems. Remove any weed or moss growth within hardscape joints. Replenish joint sand or gravel as materials migrate. Quality hardscaping will enhance your landscape for decades with periodic maintenance and diligent winter preparation.

By thoughtfully replacing portions of high-maintenance lawns with functional, decorative hardscapes, you can gain expanded living space, greater design interest, and less upkeep. Gradually convert underutilized lawn into a coordinated landscape showcasing the home's architecture through cohesive hardscape installations. The increased enjoyment, property value, and curb appeal are well worth the investment.

Chapter 7
Lawn Care Business

7.1 - Developing a Business Plan

For lawn and landscape professionals looking to start their own business, one of the key initial steps is crafting a well-thought-out business plan. This document outlines important details like your business concept, market analysis, startup costs, operations plan, and financial projections. Investing time upfront to research and develop a robust plan establishes a roadmap to guide your new venture and provides credibility when seeking loans or investors.

Executive Summary

Briefly summarize your company's mission, objectives, competitive advantages, management team strengths, and projected growth and profitability. This overview section hooks the reader and summarizes the core business pitch.

Business Description

Provide detailed information on your company's nature, focus, vision, values, and unique differentiators. Outline the specific services you will offer, the equipment and facilities needed, and the logistics of how you will deliver services. Discuss your target customer profiles and how you will market to them.

Market Analysis

Research your service area demographics, including population, median income, home ownership rates, age distribution, and other relevant statistics. Analyze competitors and companies offering similar services. Outline your competitive advantages regarding pricing, quality, experience, specializations, and customer service.

Management Team

Introduce yourself and any business partners, highlighting your industry experience, special expertise, education, and strengths. If you need more direct field experience , detail how you will bring in advisors or employees with the required skills and knowledge.

Operations Plan

Describe day-to-day processes involved in delivering services efficiently and profitably, including staffing, equipment, supplies, scheduling, and communications. Outline purchasing and supplier relationships. Discuss quality control procedures and methods for scaling operations up. Provide projections for start-up costs, operating expenses, and revenues. Startup costs include equipment purchases, insurance, facilities, licensing, marketing, and other expenses accrued before opening. Estimate operating expenses like payroll, fuel, maintenance, insurance, supplies, and professional fees. Forecast sales and revenue based on projected client contracts and jobs.

Include forecasts for cash flow, income statements, and balance sheets. Perform break-even analysis to determine sales volumes needed to reach profitability. Detail assumptions and formulas used in financial modeling projections. Identify risks like seasonality, rain delays, and gas prices that could impact finances. Outline your desired profit margin and pricing strategy.

Funding Requirements

Specify precisely how much funding you need, expected sources, and how the funds will be used. Common options are business loans, personal savings, investments from partners, or loans from friends and family. Document precise use of funds such as equipment purchases, insurance, facilities, inventory, marketing, permitting.

Implementation Timeline

Outline specific action steps and target dates required to launch your business. Allocate timeframes for securing funding, purchasing equipment, establishing office space, hiring staff, training, licensing, marketing, and all essential startup tasks. Build in a contingency buffer for delays.

Appendix

Include supporting documents like licenses and permits, owner resumes, market research data, letters of reference, sample marketing materials, and other relevant information to substantiate the plan.

With careful research, analysis, and planning, a comprehensive business plan provides a roadmap for successfully launching your lawn and landscape company on a solid foundation.

7.2 - Licensing & Insurance

Before operating a lawn or landscape business, it is essential to ensure you have the proper licensing, registrations, and insurance coverage in place. Adhering to state and local legal requirements protects your company and provides credibility when marketing services. Working without adequate insurance leaves you financially vulnerable to equipment damage, property damage, injuries, and customer claims. Taking time upfront to research and obtain necessary credentials, licenses, and policies reduces risk and instills professional confidence.

First, decide on a formal business structure - the most common options are sole proprietorship, partnership, corporation, or LLC. Each has different tax and legal implications. Incorporating or forming an LLC provides personal liability protection but costs more to establish. As a sole proprietor or partner, you'll be taxed on business income under personal tax returns.

Research specific licenses your state and municipality require for operating a landscaping business. Common credentials are a state business license, nursery stock dealer license, pesticide applicator license, local business permit, and sales tax permit. Maintain proper certifications for employees applying pesticides or operating heavy equipment. Allow sufficient lead time for studying for and obtaining licenses before starting operations.

Purchase robust, tailored insurance coverage to protect your business. Recommended policies include general liability, which covers property damage and bodily injury claims by others against your business; commercial auto to protect vehicles used for business purposes; workers' compensation, which is required in most states to cover medical and lost wage costs for on-the-job employee injuries; commercial property to insure tools, equipment, supplies and office space against damage, theft and natural disasters; E&O to cover financial harm to clients from errors or omissions by your company; and umbrella liability for additional liability limits beyond underlying policies.

Consult knowledgeable insurance agents to review appropriate coverages, limits, and deductibles given the size and scope of your business and services provided. Having the proper licenses and insurance in place legitimizes your business while protecting your company assets and reducing personal liability. Renew policies on time and keep compliance documentation available when required. Some states require landscaping businesses to obtain a contractor's bond, which provides financial protection if you fail to meet contractual obligations. Bonds can also help win bids for big commercial projects. Check your state and local requirements regarding contractor bond needs.

Hiring Employees

When hiring staff, verify they have any required trade licenses or pesticide applicator certifications. Conduct drug tests and background checks, especially for employees driving vehicles or operating equipment. Have employees sign non-compete and confidentiality agreements to protect your business interests.

Post legal notices like required labor law and OSHA safety posters in your office. Consult the IRS about tax withholding, submittal of payroll taxes, and providing W-2s to employees. Depending on staff size, you may need worker's compensation and unemployment insurance. Stay current on all labor, safety, and tax regulations affecting your workers.

Facility & Vehicle Registration

Register your business address and storage yards with the state and obtain local approval for signage. Title and register vehicles in your business name. Place company information on vehicles according to DOT regulations. Follow requirements for trailer licensing, inspection, titling, and registration.

Proper documentation, licensing, and insurance protocol protect your company, demonstrate credibility, meet legal obligations, and give customers confidence in your professionalism. Keep licenses current through renewals and maintain adequate insurance levels as your business evolves.

7.3 - Estimating Jobs

Creating accurate estimates is a critical skill for operating a profitable landscaping business. Your estimates establish clear project scope and specifications for clients while covering your expenses and profit margin. Rushing through estimating without understanding the complete work scope leads to underestimating, which erodes profits over time. Invest time upfront in careful estimating to bid jobs confidently while avoiding unexpected costs down the road.

Define Project Scope

Start by meeting with clients on-site to discuss their needs and vision while assessing all factors that will impact the work involved. Ask questions to understand timing, priorities, budget parameters, and exactly what is included in the desired scope. Determine requirements like materials, equipment access, waste removal, and any permits needed. Set clear expectations around what will and will not be addressed.

Measure Site & Quantities

Take measurements of all areas that will be worked on, including lawn square footage, bed dimensions, hardscapes, and material quantities needed. Capture any irregular shapes or site factors that go beyond basic squares and rectangles. Confirm utility locations to avoid lines during excavation or installation of signage, lighting, or irrigation systems. Use laser measuring devices for precision over pacing off areas.

Map & Document Site

Visually diagram the property layout, structures, vegetation, topography, and other permanent features influencing the work. Document with photographs and notes any existing conditions that will increase the scope, like severely overgrown beds, drainage issues, or demolished old features being replaced. Create a documented baseline to reference if any disputes arise later about original site conditions.

Research Costs

Building an accurate estimate requires researching current costs for all materials, equipment, and subcontractors required to execute the specified scope of work. Get quotes from vendors on plants, soils, hardscapes, and lumber. Review all equipment rental fees. Get subcontractor bids for any outsourced services like concrete pouring or electrical work. Confirm labor wages based on projected hours. Include projected fuel costs for operating equipment and vehicles. Identify any permit fees. Use researched costs, not outdated assumptions, when estimating. Analyze the work details and assign realistic timeframes for completing each task based on your crews' hourly production rates. Account for travel time between sites and allow buffers for incidentals and changes that arise during projects. It is better to overestimate hours than underestimate. Confirm current hourly wages for employees based on their skill level and experience. Calculate the total estimated labor by multiplying hours x hourly rate per worker.

Overhead Costs

Factor in overhead costs like equipment purchase and maintenance, insurance, licensing, office expenses, advertising, accountant fees and other operating costs. These can equal 20-50% of total job costs. Allocate a fair percentage to each job estimate to cover your fixed overhead expenses. Avoid the mindset of pricing jobs only to cover labor and materials.

Profit Margin

Add your desired profit margin with all costs calculated, typically 15-25% above expenses. The resulting total is your minimum acceptable bid amount for the defined work. Submit bids promptly while details are fresh. Follow up on estimates and clarify scope as needed. Careful estimating protects profits while building client relationships.

Change Orders

For changes in scope after project commencement, provide written change orders to detail additional costs and schedule impacts. Do not absorb extra work without documenting for payment, as this erodes job profitability. Integrate change orders into overall project billing.

Accurate job estimating is a key success factor for profitable landscape business operations. Invest time upfront, thoroughly quantifying all aspects of each job to bid competitively while avoiding cost overruns.

7.4 Advertising & Marketing

Advertising and marketing are critical components of growing a successful lawn care business. With so many competitors in the industry, you need to make your company stand out and attract new customers. Developing an effective advertising and marketing strategy takes time, creativity, and a budget, but it's an investment that will pay dividends as your customer base expands.

Starting with the basics, every lawn care business needs a logo, company colors, and a tagline to build its brand identity. Your logo should be simple and memorable, and convey a sense of professionalism and quality work. Popular color choices include green, blue, and earth tones that connect to nature, growth, and the environment. Spend time brainstorming ideas for a short, catchy tagline that captures the essence of your business, such as "We care for lawns" or "Creating healthy, beautiful lawns."

Brochures are an indispensable marketing tool, so create a professional trifold brochure right away when starting your business. Include eye-catching photos of lush, green lawns you've maintained and a list of all the services you provide. Use bullet points to highlight your experience, licensing, insurance coverage, and any specialties like organic practices. Make sure to list your contact information prominently and keep the content focused on customer benefits.

Every lawn care business also needs a website to provide detailed information and photos to prospective online clients. Either hire a web designer or use a template from a site like Wix to quickly create a modern, responsive website. Optimize the site for local SEO by including your city, service area, and relevant keywords so customers can easily find you through search engines. Remember prominent calls to action for visitors to contact you for quotes.

Google My Business, Facebook, and other social media platforms allow you to list your lawn care business so nearby customers can find and contact you. Complete your profiles thoroughly with engaging photos, service details, and customer reviews. Interact regularly by posting lawn care tips, before and after project photos, and responses to reviews and inquiries. Search engine and social media marketing establishes your web presence and helps funnel traffic to your site.

While online marketing is extremely important, pay attention to traditional options. Print ads in local newspapers and neighborhood circulars can reach homeowners, not online. Classified ads are very affordable; pay a little extra for a small logo or photo ad for maximum impact. Partner with local realtors to provide lawn care gift certificates for new homeowners. Attend community events to network and hand out brochures. Sponsor a little league team and put up a banner with your company name and logo.

Signage and vehicle lettering are great marketing that makes your business visible wherever you go. Order custom lawn signs with your logo, tagline, and phone number to place around neighborhoods when working. Get your logo and contact information professionally painted or wrapped on your trucks, trailesr, and equipment. Attractive magnetic door signs are inexpensive and easy to remove when not working.

Strategically mailed postcards and flyers are an inexpensive way to target specific neighborhoods you want to attract business from. Use a mailing service like Every Door Direct Mail for efficient distribution. Time the mailings around peak periods like spring green up and fall overseeding when customers think about their lawn care needs. Include a compelling offer like 10% off seasonal services or a free quote.

Leveraging happy customers to attract new ones through referrals is hugely valuable for a small business. Providing exemplary service that exceeds expectations greatly increases the chance of referrals. After completing a job, ask satisfied clients if they would be willing to recommend your business or provide a testimonial. Handing out referral cards can help spur sharing, as can rewards for successful referrals.

Advertising and marketing your lawn care business takes persistence and creativity, but following proven methods will build your brand, customer awareness, and income. Allocate a sufficient budget for marketing expenses and track results to optimize your strategy. In conjunction with online and traditional tactics, referral marketing will maximize growth as you build a prosperous local company. Stay flexible to take advantage of new opportunities and channels as they emerge in this digital age. With dedication and smart marketing, you can grow a distinctive, thriving lawn care business. Once you've built up your client base, it's important to focus on customer retention and building relationships through stellar service and communication. Send out periodic emails with lawn care tips, service reminders, new service offerings, and occasional discounts to encourage repeat business. Customers who are happy with your work and hear from you regularly are much more likely to use you again and refer others.

Surveys are a simple way to get feedback and identify areas for improvement. A short email survey after a service asks customers to rate things like quality, timeliness, communication, and overall satisfaction. This allows you to benchmark performance and quickly address any complaints. Following up with an occasional phone call check-in to your best customers can further strengthen ties when you ask about their lawn, offer advice, and remind them to reach out for future needs.

While growing through new customers is important, selling additional services to existing clients has higher success rates and lower costs. Once they're happy with your mowing and basic care, propose extra services like fertilization, aeration, irrigation, landscape design, hardscaping, tree trimming, and more. Send out promotions for new services you're highlighting each month. Cross-selling expands wallet share and strengthens retention.

To encourage repeat business year after year:
Offer annual lawn care service packages.
Bundle together services like mowing, fertilizing, aerating, and overseeding at a discounted rate compared to buying individually.
Send an email reminder when it's time for customers to renew their annual plan with you.
Offer multiple tiers like basic, advanced, and premium packages at different price points to suit varying needs.

Rewarding loyalty is always a good business practice. After a customer has remained with you for a full year or season, give a token of appreciation like a gift card or complimentary extra service. Launch a referral rewards program that gives a discount or free service credit to both the referring and new customer. Loyalty programs recognize your best customers and keep them coming back.

As your business grows, you may need to bring on employees, either part-time seasonal help or full-time workers. Finding good talent can be challenging, so get the word out in multiple ways. Place help-wanted ads in local papers and online job boards highlighting your great work environment and growth opportunities. Partner with landscaping programs at nearby vocational schools and community colleges to hire recent graduates. Ask your network for referrals of promising candidates.

Once you have workers on board, invest in thorough training on proper techniques, safety protocols, customer service, and your specific approach to quality work. Set clear expectations for performance and schedule regular check-ins to provide feedback. Incentivize through competitive pay, performance bonuses, and rewards programs. A solid training foundation and engaged employees will be a major asset.

Managing the day-to-day operations of a growing lawn care business takes foresight and organization. Establish efficient processes for scheduling jobs, routing crews, managing inventory, and invoicing. Keep a close eye on cash flow and projection. Continue networking with other small business owners to learn best practices. Consider bringing on a business manager or consultant if you need high-level assistance. Staying on top of the business side allows you to focus on providing great service.

Revisit your business plan each year to set new objectives and strategies for continued growth. Set specific goals for revenue, number of customers, service expansion, equipment investments, hiring needs, and other metrics. Identify emerging opportunities in the market, like sustainability services, or potential threats, like new competitors. Use your updated plan as a roadmap for the next stage of strategic growth.

At some point, you will max out the volume of customers you can properly serve at your current business size. Expanding to multiple crews and additional trucks/equipment allows you to take on more jobs and new neighborhoods. Bring on a general manager to oversee operations teams and field staff if needed. While rapid growth requires upfront investments, the long-term gains in profitability and market share are substantial when executed well.

Bring in trusted advisors for major operational changes like expansion, diversification or acquisitions. Your accountant can assess tax implications of growth and impact on finances. A business lawyer can guide you through the legal aspects of new ventures, employees, regulations, and more. A marketing expert can help plot promotion strategies to attract more customers. The input of professionals minimizes risk and prevents avoidable missteps.

Diversifying your services beyond basic lawn care also presents growth opportunities once your core business is thriving. Offer landscape design and installation services for patios, walkways, ponds, lighting systems, and more to increase sales. Expand into tree care services like pruning, removal, stump grinding, and planting. Snow and ice removal in winter provide year-round income. Establishing vertical services allows you to capture more value.

You can build an extremely successful local lawn care business with a dedication to quality work, smart marketing, and strategic growth planning. Constantly look for ways to improve operations, take on new services, retain happy customers, and expand your reach. The opportunities to grow a prosperous company in this vital industry are only limited by your vision, innovation, and willingness to take strategic risks that pay off. By providing a great service and adapting to market changes, your business can continue thriving well into the future.

7.5 Managing Employees:

As your lawn care business grows, you will likely need to bring on employees to help handle the increasing workload. Effectively managing workers is critical for providing consistent, high-quality service to your growing customer base. There are many factors to consider when building your team.

Staffing needs depend on the scale of your operations and how much work you aim to take on. Carefully assess labor requirements during peak seasons like spring and fall when customer demand spikes. For basic mowing and maintenance routes, plan for one employee per 8-10 residential lawn accounts as a manageable workload. More complex properties and commercial sites take longer, requiring more staffing per account.

When hiring, seek a mix of full-time workers interested in long-term roles and part-time seasonal help to meet summer and fall peaks. Clearly convey the physical nature of the work during recruitment so expectations are set. Look for safety-focused team players with landscaping experience and a commitment to service quality. Check references thoroughly.

Onboarding and training new hires are crucial to building an effective workforce. Review your company policies, safety protocols, and service processes in detail. Educate them on the proper use of equipment and tools. Shadow experienced employees on routes to learn site-specific needs and techniques. Instill your quality standards through hands-on training. Periodically evaluate skills and provide more training to improve any deficiencies. Proper onboarding prevents problems down the road.

To motivate your team:
Establish fair compensation benchmarked to industry averages and local conditions.
Pay your best employees well to retain them long-term.
Consider performance pay increases, bonuses for safety records, and incentives for completing training certifications.

Small perks like company shirts, paid time off, and lunch on Fridays also boost morale. Reward your top performers both financially and with recognition.

Tracking hours precisely is critical for payroll accuracy. Set up processes for employees to easily log daily hours, whether on routes or other tasks. Confirm totals weekly. For field staff, consider using a mobile app for clocking in from sites or having the office enter hours from submitted route sheets. Maintain tidy payroll records and comply with all reporting requirements. Accurate timekeeping avoids future hassles.

Keep your workforce productive and engaged through effective scheduling and communication. Use a master calendar to assign staff, equipment, and vehicles to daily client routes. Stagger start times to align with typical heavy mowing hours. Schedule maintenance, meetings, and training during slower mid-day windows. Maintain open lines of communication so you can adjust schedules as needed.

Provide employees with all necessary equipment and supplies to efficiently complete their work each day. This includes properly maintained mowers, trimmers, blowers, safety gear, and a full stock of gas, oil, lawn products, and parts. Monitor inventory and service equipment regularly. Missing items or tools quickly hurts productivity. Make sure support systems like scheduling and payroll are running smoothly.

Training continues beyond just initial onboarding. Hold regular tailgate meetings where crews gather to discuss challenges, safety issues, client feedback, and process improvements. Arrange for manufacturers or distributors to provide equipment operation and maintenance clinics. Send supervisors to seminars on leadership skills. Ongoing training sharpens skills and provides advancement opportunities.

Gathering input from employees helps identify issues and fosters engagement. Maintain an open door policy for workers to offer suggestions or raise concerns anytime. Schedule monthly or quarterly meetings focused specifically on discussing ideas for improvement. Ask for honest feedback via periodic anonymous surveys to gauge job satisfaction, workload, and other factors. Acting on this input improves operations.

Providing excellent working conditions and culture builds loyalty and retention. Make safety an utmost priority through proper protocols, protective equipment, training and monitoring. Support work/life balance with policies like flexible schedules when possible. Create opportunities for team building and staff recognition. Respect your employees and they will respect you and your customers.

Managing payroll, compliance, scheduling, training, and other human resource tasks can become complex as your workforce grows. Consider bringing on an HR manager or using an HR firm. Their expertise in regulations, reporting, and best practices is well worth the investment. They can also manage recruiting, performance management, and other key functions so you can focus elsewhere.

As the owner, you set the tone for your lawn care business. Lead by example through your strong work ethic, integrity with customers and suppliers, and willingness to tackle any task. Employees follow your cultural cues, so exhibit the conduct you expect from your team. Investment in building a skilled, dedicated workforce pays dividends for years to come. Supervising and evaluating your workforce is essential once you have employees on board. Assign clear roles and responsibilities to each worker and hold them accountable. Ride along on routes periodically to check workmanship and identify needs for improvement through coaching. Track efficiency metrics like lawns serviced per man-hour. Nip any performance issues in the bud before they become major problems.

Formal performance reviews conducted annually or biannually provide important feedback opportunities. Gather input from supervisors and colleagues as part of 360-degree feedback. Set goals and create development plans for advancement. Adjust compensation based on skill gains, work volumes, and market rates. Documentation protects you legally if disciplinary action is ever required.

Speaking of legal obligations, comply fully with all labor regulations in your region. Pay at least minimum wage and time-and-a-half for overtime per federal laws. For temporary seasonal staff, check rules regarding worker classification and payroll taxes. Adhere to discrimination, leave of absence, safety, and other rules governing workers. Consult a lawyer if HR issues arise.

While your core field staff are critical assets, you also recognize the value of quality administrative help in the office. Hire or outsource bookkeeping, customer service, scheduling, and other back-office functions so you can focus on operations. An experienced office manager oversees these teams and keeps your business running smoothly.

Managing subcontractors requires a different approach than employees. Rather than supervising their work directly, vet subcontractors thoroughly upfront based on certifications, equipment, experience, and references. Check for required licenses and insurance coverage. Draw up contracts covering schedule, quality standards, work rates, and terms for adding services and either party terminating the agreement.

Schedule subcontractor services during your peak demand periods as needed. Communicate job details and requirements clearly. Make sure they adhere to your safety protocols and represent your brand professionally to customers. Monitor periodically to ensure they deliver quality up to your standards. Having trusted subcontractors supplements your workforce at busy times.

Some lawn care companies choose to bring certain services in-house as they grow rather than subcontracting them long-term. For example, you may acquire trucks and staff to handle irrigation system installation instead of using an outside specialty provider. This requires upfront investments but allows you to control quality and pricing. Weigh the pros and cons of outsourcing vs. insourcing key services as your needs change over time.

No matter how great your processes are, interpersonal issues can crop up in any workplace. Personality conflicts, disagreements over workloads, and issues with management – handling these problems before they escalate maintains team cohesion. Be transparent about policies, offer mediation if needed, and remain impartial when assessing facts. Protect privacy and avoid playing favorites.

Similarly, know how to spot and address potential substance abuse issues early through fair warning and offers of counseling support. Safety is too critical in this industry to ignore warning signs. Don't allow personal problems impacting work to go unaddressed. Be understanding but firm in requiring professional conduct on the job.

For serious conflicts, disciplinary protocols are warranted. Verbally warn employees about their unacceptable conduct, then follow up with a written warning if there is no improvement. For major violations, consider either temporary unpaid suspension or complete termination as needed to remedy the situation. Involve HR support and follow consistent processes to avoid wrongful actions.

When the unfortunate need to let someone go arises, handle it with humanity while protecting the company. Review the rationale with a lawyer in advance for guidance. Break the news to the employee in a private conversation. Offer a severance package if feasible. Don't discuss details with others and confirm the worker's final pay and benefits. Part respectfully.

While building and leading a team has challenges, the upside of leveraging employees to grow your business makes the effort worthwhile. Workers who feel valued and take pride in their contributions will go the extra mile for you and your customers. Make staffing decisions strategically based on workload, budgets, and service needs as you scale up operations. With the right team behind you, the possibilities are endless.

Managing the myriad responsibilities of running a thriving lawn care business takes time, to master. Consider finding a mentor – either within your network or through a program – who can offer guidance and support from their own experiences building a successful service company. Their real-world wisdom can help you avoid pitfalls as your business enters new stages of growth.

7.6 Expanding Services:

Once your core lawn care business thrives, offering additional services represents a logical pathway for growth and increased profitability. Options like landscaping design and enhancements, tree care, snow removal, and more allow you to diversify your income streams while leveraging your existing client base. With careful planning, expanding what you offer can take your company to the next level.

Start by surveying current customers about what extra services they would be interested in purchasing from your business. Gauge the demand for offerings like irrigation installation, landscape lighting, hardscaping, drainage solutions, and seasonal services such as gutter cleaning or holiday lighting. This market research will point you toward the most viable opportunities worth pursuing.

Research competitor offerings and pricing for the services you are considering before deciding what to add. Look for gaps in the local market where customer needs are not being fully met. Your business can carve out a niche around sustainable practices, superior design eye, or designing services uniquely. Choose new offerings strategically based on your strengths and customer priorities.

Analyze the operational impact of adding services carefully before jumping in. How much new staff, training, equipment, marketing spend, and other resources will be required? Do you have the proper in-house expertise, or should the service be subcontracted initially? Gauge how service expansions will affect your existing business workflows and bandwidth. Take a phased approach if needed to smooth major transitions.

Some diversifications, like irrigation or lighting, require specific technical skills and special equipment. Invest in comprehensive hands-on training for your staff – either through a vendor, manufacturer, or trade school. Hire subcontractors or qualified employees to properly handle more complex installations and upgrades until your team gains proficiency. Do not compromise quality as you build expertise.

Upgrading tools and fleet vehicles is likely needed when adding new services. Research the costs and lifespan of equipment. Buy quality commercial-grade gear that improves productivity and minimizes breakdowns. For major purchases, look into equipment financing options that preserve capital. Provide adequate facilities and storage for housing expanded fleet assets securely.

Modifying existing facilities or adding new physical locations may be prudent, depending on growth plans. Construct additional garage bays for housing vehicles. Install secure fenced storage areas for materials. If expanding to multiple regions, consider opening satellite offices closer to certain customer bases to improve efficiency. Factor in facility needs well in advance before launching new offerings.

Updating your business permitting and licensing is required when diversifying services. Research legal requirements for each area you plan to expand into. Apply for necessary state and local permits, licenses, and insurance coverage additions early in the planning process to avoid delays. Consult attorneys and government offices to ensure you meet every requirement before offering new services.

Strategic market research helps determine which service expansions make the most sense for your current customer base. Survey clients about their level of interest in potential new offerings and how much they currently spend on those services. Gauge where they feel their needs are not completely satisfied by competitors. Collecting solid data minimizes the risk of introducing services for which there is little demand.

Another smart technique for minimizing risk with new service launches is piloting first. Try rolling out a new offering across a small subset of existing clients to gauge adoption and refine processes before a full launch. Work out any kinks on a small scale through a pilot test rather than betting your full business on an untried service area.

Proper staffing is essential when adding business lines to ensure workmanship meets your quality bar. Bring on specialists if needed for highly skilled services until your current team can be cross-trained. Reassess labor requirements in each area and adjust staffing levels accordingly. Be selective when hiring additional employees to support growth. Don't compromise on talent. When launching new services , dedicated marketing and sales efforts are required to generate customer awareness and adoption. Create customized print and digital collateral clearly explaining your expanded capabilities. Highlight how bundling services creates convenience and value. Offer bundled service discounts and other promotions to incentivize trials. Getting the word out properly ensures new branches gain traction.

Track metrics carefully across both existing and new business lines to gauge performance. Look at revenue, profitability margins, customer acquisition costs, adoption rates, workforce productivity, customer satisfaction, and other KPIs specific to each service. Ensure new offerings are achieving target benchmarks and supporting healthy overall growth. Adjust strategies based on data insights.

Be prepared to patiently nurture new services through sometimes lengthy ramp-up periods before they produce desired returns. Invest adequately upfront in essential infrastructure, skills training, marketing, and staffing to set the growth foundations. Recognize new offerings may operate at a loss initially. Stick with your expansion plan as long as data shows actual promise building.

Remain vigilant about potential cannibalization of existing services when diversifying your offerings. If new branches steal business away from established areas that are performing well, reconsider your overall strategic balance. Services should complement each other to provide customers full solutions rather than undercutting profitable legacy workstreams.

Keep looking for additional expansion opportunities even after entering new spaces. As you conquer a niche, new needs you could fill often become apparent. Let one successful diversification pave the way for assessing further areas to grow. Diversified lawn care companies offering "one-stop-shops" hold an advantage in customer convenience.

If the numbers make sense, buying an established company in your region with complementary services represents another rapid growth tactic.. Acquisitions allow you to immediately assimilate their customer base, market share, and competencies. But be wary of major post-merger integration challenges across leadership, culture, systems, and processes, and factor risks into valuation models.

Growth through franchising is a route some lawn care companies take, granting regional franchises the right to operate under their brand using proven systems. This scales quickly through distributed ownership but requires extensive operations documentation and support. Weigh the pros and cons of franchising vs. company-owned units for your goals. Standardization and quality control are challenges.

To fuel aggressive expansion plans, explore different approaches to financing beyond traditional loans and lines of credit. Private equity investment provides large capital infusions for rapid growth in exchange for partial ownership. Mezzanine debt offers flexible repayment terms tailored to projected cashflows. Leverage multiple sources strategically.

Updating business financial models is imperative before undertaking major expansions. Build detailed assumptions into projected cash flow statements based on costs of new hires, facilities, equipment, marketing, and other ramp-up investments. Scrutinize effects on profitability targets. Update breakeven points and inventory needs. Conservative modeling protects against nasty surprises.

Resist spreading yourself too thin by diversifying into too many peripheral areas at once. Attempting to launch and scale numerous new services simultaneously diverts focus, strains resources, and carries substantial risk. Pursue only a couple of thoughtful expansions in a given timeframe. Move to the next phase deliberately, not by overeager reaction.

As you evaluate entering new arenas, be mindful of potential future threats.. How will emerging technologies like robotic landscaping equipment impact labor needs? Are demographic shifts in your region favoring certain offerings more than others? Could a newly merged mega-competitor threaten your market share? Let your strategic roadmap address visible obstacles on the horizon so you remain agile and competitive.

Growing an assortment of profitable services unified under your professional brand elevates your company's stature and customer appeal. But avoid diluting branding by diversifying into too many disjointed areas unrelated to your core competencies. Expand thoughtfully into spaces where your expertise offers real added value. With balance across change and focus, significant growth opportunities await.

Chapter 8
Lawn Pests

8.1 Weed Identification:

Weeds are unwelcome intruders on any lawn. Managing common weed types through proper identification, prevention, and control measures is an ongoing battle for home gardeners and professionals alike. Knowing your weed adversaries is half the battle when it comes to protecting lush, pristine turfgrass.

The most prevalent annual warm-season weeds plaguing lawns are crabgrass, foxtail, and spurge. Crabgrass is arguably the most troublesome due to its quick germination and spreading through surface stolons. Its most identifiable feature is two distinctly parallel leaves on hairless stems. Foxtail weeds disrupt uniformity with their bushy vertical seed heads. Spotted spurge sprouts pinkish flowers and a mat of oblong leaves on prostrate stems from late spring into fall.

Dandelions are the classic cool-season perennial weed thriving in home lawns everywhere. Their stubborn taproots frustrate gardeners who think removal efforts are successfu,l only to see fresh yellow flowers and jagged leaves reemerge again and again. Other cool-season perennials like creeping Charlie, clover, and ground ivy similarly employ vigorous underground root systems to their survival advantage.

Nutsedge weeds produce funnel-shaped foliage and wiry rhizomes that weave extensively, causing rapid spreading. Yellow nutsedge and the less common purple nutsedge can take over lawns in warm climates within just a couple of seasons. Their tubers and roots penetrate deep into soil, making it extremely difficult to eradicate nutsedge permanently.

Knowing whether a weed is a grassy or broadleaf type is helpful for proper control measures. Grassy weeds share similarities with desirable lawn grasses and often prove harder to selectively eliminate without damaging the surrounding turf. Crabgrass, foxtail, nimblewill, and annual bluegrass are examples of common grassy intruders. Broadleaf weeds have more distinct foliage features that differentiate them from grasses for more targeted chemical control.

Quackgrass is a notoriously aggressive perennial grassy weed for northern lawns. Featuring long tapered blades and vigorous rhizomes, quackgrass grows in thick patches that can crowd out entire sections of desired turfgrass. Its tenacious nature earns it a spot on any most wanted list for weed controls. Proper identification is crucial in dealing with the unique challenges of quackgrass.

Chickweed, or starweed, plagues many lawns with its weedy stems, pointed oval leaves, and white star-shaped flowers. A cool-season annual, chickweed germinates successfully in thatch-filled lawns, spreading rapidly into patchy infestations. While shallow-rooted, its mat-like growth habit allows chickweed to thrive despite regular mowing of surrounding turfgrass. Timely pre-emergent and post-emergent applications provide the best chickweed prevention.

Spurge weeds demonstrate an immense talent for germinating in thin, less vigorous lawn areas. There are several annual Spurge varieties, including prostrate, spotted, and petty that can aggressively displace desirable turfgrass. All produce a toxic milky sap when stem tissue is broken. The key identification feature of spotted Spurge is distinguishable pink flowers and red-spotted foliage. Proper mowing, watering, fertilizing, and pre-emergent controls limit Spurge's foothold in healthy lawns.

Wild violet is a common broadleaf perennial weed identifiable by its oval leaves with heart-shaped bases and unique purple flowers. Also called creeping violet, its spreading rhizomes help it persist and spread through lawns, appearing as scattered individual plants or clusters. Wild violet thrives in moist, shady areas. Selective broadleaf herbicides containing triclopyr work well on established wild violet, but multiple applications are typically needed for complete control due to its extensive root system.

Mouse-ear chickweed is one of the more frequent chickweed species plaguing home lawns and sports fields, particularly in wet, cool conditions. Its petite low growth prevents mouse-ear chickweed from being eliminated by routine mowing. Look for its defining small, furry, oval-shaped leaves paired along the central stem to distinguish mouse-ear chickweed from other common lawn weeds. Some pre-emergent and post-emergent herbicide applications provide suppression, but mouse-ear chickweed is notoriously herbicide-resistant. weeds are a common broadleaf perennial pest with wide oval leaves featuring parallel veins converging at the base. Buckhorn plantain and the similar broadleaf plantain thrive in compacted, poorly draining soils, reproducing via seeds and plant fragments. Unique upright seed stalks stand out as they mature. Plantain is difficult to selectively eliminate from lawns chemically without causing damage.

Oxalis, also called wood sorrel or creeping wood sorrel, inhabits thin grassy areas and bare soil patches throughout landscapes. Its clover-like leaves fold downward at night. Small yellow flowers stand out against the foliage. Oxalis spreads aggressively through underground bulbs and stems that root at joints when buried by mowing. Pre-emergents and post-emergents containing triclopyr provide effective oxalis control.

Common chickweed is one of the most prevalent annual weeds; its small oval leaves, white star-shaped flowers, and mat-forming habits disrupt lawn uniformity. Shallow roots make it easy to hand-pull small patches. But for heavy infestations, chickweed-specific herbicides or early pre-emergent applications work better to prevent mass germination. Spot-treating weedy areas after proper identification limits the need for broadcast applications.

Ground ivy, or creeping Charlie, creates headaches with its vigorous creeping and low-growing nature that resists mowing. Kidney-shaped fused leaves with scalloped margins form dense mats. Blue funnel-shaped flowers appear in spring. This perennial broadleaf weed thrives in moist, shady spots. Chemical controls aim to damage its extensive root system and limit regrowth. Some products now target ground ivy specifically.

Wild garlic and wild onion are not technically weeds, but bulbs and leaves of these aggressive Allium species disrupt desired turfgrasses in home lawns and sports fields. The fresh-cut-grass scent emanating from underfoot brushes confirms identification. Pulling often leaves remnants that resprout. Repeated selective herbicide applications starting in early spring help control the growth and spread of wild allium bulbs.

Shepherd's purse is a prolific annual weed across lawns, landscapes, and agricultural fields. Its identifying features include a flat rosette basal leaf formation and multiple tiny white flowers clustered at the top of each stem. Prolific seed production fuels its fast colonization. Timely pre-emergents limit germination of shepherd's purse, while post-emergents containing 2,4-D and dicamba provide chemical control options.

Yellow woodsorrel, also called oxalis, irritates lawn owners with its low-growing clover-like foliage and underground bulbs that break apart easily when disturbed. Dislodged fragments spread quickly into new plants. Yellow flowers showcase their vibrant color. Specialty herbicides work well on yellow woodsorrel, but follow-up applications are usually needed to fully eradicate it due to its bulbs.

Prostrate knotweed frustrates lawn care experts with its persistent shallow roots that resist most weed control efforts. Tiny white flowers sit in leaf joints of this summer annual. Its wiry, mat-forming growth habit allows prostrate knotweed to escape being cut by mowers. Combining pre-emergent and post-emergent herbicides offers the best odds of limiting its foothold in struggling lawns.

Goosegrass is a summer annual grassy weed thriving in heavily compacted, poor soil. Its grey-green color contrasts noticeably with surrounding turfgrass. Two tiny claw-like appendages hug each seed, giving goosegrass its identifiable features once mature. Heavy infestations indicate soil problems needing remedy. Pre-emergent controls such as prodiamine prevent most goosegrass if timed properly in spring.

Common purslane plagues vegetable gardens and thinner lawn areas with fleshy, prostrate foliage forming flat mats. Smooth, succulent upright stems and tiny yellow flowers sit close to the ground. This annual weed favors poor, dry soils. Pre-emergents inhibit purslane's seed germination before it takes hold. Post-emergents work best when plants are small. Wear gloves when handling, as purslane sap can cause skin irritation.

8.2 Insect Identification:

A variety of insect pests can wreak havoc on pristine lawns if not properly identified and controlled. Learning to recognize the most common lawn invaders and their signs of damage is the first step toward effective pest management. Some insects harm grass directly, while others merely detract from aesthetics.

Grubs, especially white grubs, are among the most destructive insects infesting lawns. In the larval life stage of beetles such as Japanese beetle, June beetle, or chafers, white grubs chew through the grass roots, leading to dead patches. Identifying them when digging up sod samples indicates the need for grub control measures. Their C-shaped white bodies are easy to spot against soil and roots.

Ants tunneling through lawns signify potential pest problems below. While ants cause minimal direct damage, their trails signal the presence of other insects, including aphids or soft scales on roots which ants tend for honeydew secretions. Trails leading to bare or thinning patches warrant further investigation. Proper ant species identification provides clues to their role.

Chinch bugs are a nemesis for homeowners trying to grow thick, healthy lawns, especially in hot climates. The small insects extract juices from grass blades and thatch while injecting enzymes that destroy turf. Damaged areas appear dried out with yellowish to brown dead patches. Close inspection reveals the pinhead-sized insects clustering at the base of grass stems.

Sod webworms produce lawn damage resembling drought stress, but their signs are limited to circular patches. Pulling back on the edges of these spots reveals caterpillars and webbing in the thatch. Treatment with insecticides such as carbaryl or halofenozide provides optimum prevention when applied early as young larvae begin feeding on grass blades. Proper identification starts with recognizing their unique damage patterns.

Cutworms are aptly named for their habit of damaging lawn grass and garden plants by chewing through stems at or below soil level. Several cutworm species can attack turf, but symptoms are similar. Irregular bare patches appear, sometimes containing severed grass shoots. Digging near the damage exposes plump caterpillar larvae up to 2 inches long, responsible for the cutting. These night-feeding pests require diligent monitoring to catch.

Armyworms derive their name from their distinct habit of marching en masse across turf areas, devouring grass blades in their wake. These 2-inch long striped caterpillars leave behind patches of closely cropped brown grass as evidence. Careful inspection of damaged areas reveals the bristly larvae to confirm identification. Quick-killing insecticides, diazinon, or carbaryl stop them before extensive devastation.

Leafhoppers are tiny, carrot-shaped insects named for their propensity to leap rapidly when foliage is disturbed. While they feed from grass blades, leafhopper damage is minimal. However, these common insects are symptomatic of environments favoring other pests and diseases. Monitoring helps determine if controls are warranted based on developing threats beyond leafhoppers alone. Sticky traps aid population sampling.

Slugs and snails leave telltale signs of their presence on grass plants, including holes chewed in foliage and shiny mucous trails on blades, thatch, and hard surfaces. These soft-bodied gastropods feed more actively at night. Regular soap water drenches offer organic control. Quick elimination is essential as substantial slime buildup detracts from lawn appearance. Identification of shiny trails or slime confirms the culprits.

Billbug adults cause little direct injury, but their legless larvae burrow into stems and crowns of grass plants, eventually destroying them. Infestations become visible as patches of discolored, dying turf. Adult billbugs can often be spotted on their sides with legs curled if overturned. Larval sampling and damage assessment indicate optimal billbug treatment timing to minimize loss. Correct identification is vital for ideal control. Cicadas rank among the most unmistakable lawn pests with their large size, distinctive wing noise, and sheer numbers emerging in periodic cycles. While adults cause little feeding damage, egg-laying damage to tree limbs can allow disease entry points. Their cacophonous mating calls annoy homeowners. Cicada identification is easy, but predicting emergence years is key for control preparations.

Fall armyworms migrate northward each summer in large swarms that can suddenly devastate grass and crop plants. Voracious nighttime feeding leaves lawns looking ragged and chewed to the crown. Masses of dark 1.5-inch long caterpillars with light striping identify these pests upon inspection. Quick treatment with synthetic pyrethroids offers the best protection of turfgrass once correctly identified.

Scarab beetle grubs, including Japanese beetles, June beetles, masked chafers, and others, damage lawns by feeding on roots. Their C-shaped white larvae cause yellowing areas, which can be peeled back easily to reveal grubs. Adults emerge to feed on plant foliage and do little harm to grass. Timely applications of grub-targeting insecticides such as trichlorfon provide control based on signs of grub activity.

Mites are tiny arthropods related to spiders that pierce plant cells and suck out contents. Clover and gall mites cause minor aesthetic damage to lawn grass. Their microscopic size requires a hand lens or microscope to properly identify species. Mite feeding weakens the grass and causes stippling. Light leaf bronzing indicates their presence before populations explode. Judicious miticide use is only warranted for moderate infestations.

Chinch bugs attack the base of grass plants in hot, dry conditions and heavy thatch. Adults and nymphs have black bodies with white wings featuring a triangular black spot. They congregate near soil level at the edges of damaged yellowed areas. Careful inspection is required for confirmation where chinch bug treatment is needed. Targeted insecticide applications provide control before widespread habitat death.

Root aphids and other piercing-sucking insects extract plant juices and inject toxins, distorting root growth. Under warm conditions, root aphids reproduce rapidly. Aboveground symptoms include stunted turfgrass, thinning, and slowed growth. Checking soil and roots around affected areas determines if root feeders are responsible. Appropriate systemic insecticides applied early prevent major damage once pests are identified.

Ticks inhabit lawns as juveniles before maturing into blood-seeking adults. While young ticks pose little direct threat, their presence indicates areas likely to have Lyme disease-bearing deer ticks. Checking for small, sesame seed-sized nymphs determines if control measures are warranted around play areas. Removing leaf litter and proper identification help steer proactive tick management.

Crane flies resemble giant mosquitoes but are harmless, although their long legs and erratic flying alarm some homeowners. While crane fly larvae feed on plant roots, their damage is negligible on healthy lawns. Treatments are rarely needed, strictly for adult crane flies. Their presence more likely indicates a suitable habitat for grubs and other insect pests requiring diligent monitoring and prevention.

Ground pearls are curious white objects up to 3 mm across, occasionally found when digging in lawns. They are formed by ground pearl scale insects feeding on roots. Despite their name, ground pearls don't harm grass. The scales' waxy spherical coverings only indicate optimal growing conditions for other potential lawn pests worth scouting for. There is no need to treat ground pearls themselves.

Stinging ants defend nest mounds built in lawns, delivering painful bites when disturbed. Common black ants rarely harm grass itself beyond minor nest disruption. Keeping nests away from high-traffic areas through relocation or chemical treatment provides comfort. Identification of species such as fire ants determines if extensive control measures are needed to protect people, pets, and plants from aggressive stinging or biting.

8.3 Disease Identification:

Like any living organism, lawn grass is susceptible to diseases that can attack its health and aesthetics. Proper identification of symptoms leads to accurate diagnosis of causative pathogens, including fungi, bacteria, viruses, and nematodes. Catching diseases early maximizes treatment efficacy before extensive turf loss.

Cool-season grasses are vulnerable to a number of troublesome fungal diseases. Gray leaf spot appears as small tan lesions on blades surrounded by yellowing. When cool and humid, red thread manifests as pinkish mycelium threads at leaf tips. Leaf spots and melting out cause dieback. Careful symptom analysis reveals the specific disease for best management.

Necrotic ring spots are roughly circular dead patches up to a few feet wide, often with red-brown margins. The soil-borne fungal pathogen survives on grass roots and thatch. While no cure exists, early identification allows preventative fungicide applications to limit spread. Enhancing vigor through proper practices also lessens disease impact.

Take-all root rot inflicts heavy damage on cool-season turfgrass during prolonged mild, wet conditions. Starting as dark spots, affected areas swell, coalesce, and eventually die off when roots rot. The fungus persists in soils, reinfecting new grass emerging after dieback. Careful diagnosis based on patch expansion guides recommended fungicide programs for prevention when take-all root rot is identified.

Pythium blight poses a risk to homeowners trying to establish or overseed new lawns, especially in humid, wet weather. This fungal disease quickly causes root and crown rot, killing young seedlings. Affected grass pulls up easily from the spongy, deteriorating root zone. Identifying the characteristic greasy watersoaked lesions confirms pythium blight, so appropriate fungicides can be applied promptly.

Summer patch disease manifests in warmer seasons as reddish-brown circles ranging from just a few inches to several feet across. Roots under diseased areas rot away, with blades pulling loose easily. Early diagnosis of symptoms allows preventative fungicide applications to limit spread. Correct identification is key, as drought stress can resemble summer patch damage if the fungus presence goes unconfirmed.

Rhizoctonia leaf and sheath spot presents first as small dark brown spots on blades, which then spread into larger lesions mostly confined to the leaf sheaths. The fungal disease thrives under warm, humid conditions, spreading through irrigation water splash. Careful inspection reveals the stubborn pathogen for appropriate fungicide treatment before significant turf decline.

Slime molds constitute a group of primitive organisms, rather than true fungi, that colonize lawn leaf blades under warm, humid conditions. Their slimy spore masses can cover large turf areas, alarming homeowners. But slime molds cause no permanent damage. Identifying these diagnostic crusty deposits provides reassurance, as they disappear harmlessly within a few weeks as moisture levels fall.

Fairly common in southern lawns, large patch disease features yellow rings up to 20 feet wide composed of dead grass. The fungus infects leaf sheaths, eventually killing turf. Careful diagnosis of these classic symptoms allows preventative fungicide applications starting in the fall to protect grass through the following spring infection period after pathogen identification.

Snow molds pose threats to northern lawns buried under prolonged snow cover. Pink and gray snow mold fungi thrive at cold temperatures, spreading through blades trapped against soil. Inspecting for matted tan grass with fungal blotches or smoke-like mycelium after spring snowmelt allows identification and treatment of affected areas to restore health. Warm-season turfgrasses also face numerous diseases requiring prompt identification. Brown patch causes roughly circular dead patches up to several feet wide, expanding rapidly under conducive conditions. Diagnosing brown patch early allows preventative fungicide applications to limit damage once conditions favor this prevalent disease.

Take-all patch manifests as yellow, thinning turf areas that worsen despite good care. The fungus infects roots, with blades pulling up easily. Dark runner hyphae on diseased plants confirms the take-all patch for appropriate treatment. Patch diseases require identification for effective control before substantial turf loss.

Leaf spot and crown rot are common diseases on warm-season lawns. Drechslera and Bipolaris fungi produce small dark lesions on blades that spread, while Rhizoctonia attacks roots and crowns. Careful diagnosis guides suitable fungicide selection from the wide available options.

Grey leaf spot is evident by initial small oval lesions that expand into larger dead areas. The fungal pathogen thrives under warm, humid conditions. Identifying characteristic leaf symptoms signals the need for preventative fungicide applications to curb damage on highly susceptible grass varieties.

While Dollar spot disease only damages small circles a few inches wide, overlooking it allows explosive spread. Early diagnosis of initial hourglass-shaped lesions allows timely fungicide treatment. Dollar spot symptoms stand out clearly on dew-covered grass in the morning. Catching it early prevents major turf losses.

Sting nematodes are microscopic roundworms that destroy grass roots, causing symptoms resembling drought stress, such as wilting. Other nematode species debilitate turfgrass more slowly. Identifying high numbers of nematodes in soil samples confirms the required treatments to mitigate damage before plants weaken extensively.

Hard-to-control Bermudagrass decline fungal disease presents as spreading light tan patches with darker borders studded with black fruiting bodies resembling pepper grains. Careful diagnosis guides management efforts, including fungicides and turf renovation to combat this stubborn disease. Identifying onset prevents acute turf loss.

While bacterial wilt diseases are rare in lawns, they elicit dramatic symptoms, including oozing yellow slime from cut blades. Xanthomonas bacterial pathogens spread rapidly through mowing when confirmed through lab testing. Swift treatment with copper compounds may suppress bacteria after immediate identification. Preventing spread limits damage.

Viral diseases infecting lawns are seldom identified, as no control options exist. However, verifying viruses through tissue sampling eases frustration over mysterious turf decline. Most infected lawns must simply be monitored and managed until renovation is required. A quick diagnosis provides helpful closure by identifying factors causing deterioration.

Abiotic disorders like drought injury and chemical damage mimic diseases with discolored, dying grass. However, close inspection revealing no pathogen presence points to non-biological factors requiring correction, not fungicides. Proper diagnosis saves wasting resources trying to treat problems with the wrong solutions.

Accurate identification through symptom analysis and laboratory testing determines your management response in any disease outbreak. Misdiagnosis wastes time and money on ineffective treatments. Early detection allows preventative applications to restrict damage. Consult turfgrass specialists whenever unfamiliar diseases arise requiring diagnosis for strategic response.

8.4 Animal Pests:

Animal pests ranging from underground pests to dogs and deer can wreak havoc on lawns. Identifying the perpetrators of damage allows you to implement suitable deterrents or controls appropriate for each culprit. Look for key signs pointing toward specific animals when faced with mysterious lawn injuries.

Moles excavate winding underground burrows in search of insect larvae and worms, raising linear dirt mounds across lawns. Their tunnels can heave and disrupt turfgrass root systems. Confirming mole activity guides the use of vibration devices or traps to drive them away from important lawn areas.

Voles create meandering above-ground trails 1-2 inches wide when foraging on grass leaves and stems. Populations explode in the fall before dropping off. Chewed vegetation and small burrow openings identify voles for appropriate baiting or trapping. Their damage is especially detrimental to new seedlings.

Raccoons employ their dexterous front paws to roll back sections of sod in search of tasty grubs and other soil-dwelling insects. Once a suitable food source is found, raccoons will return nightly. Large overturned areas identify raccoon grub feeding for appropriate deterrents.

Rabbits nibble on a wide variety of garden and landscape plants. In lawns, they favor soft, tender, new growth, chewing grass blades down to the crown, which damages developing turf. Identifying irregular patches of clipped vegetation points to night-feeding rabbits as the culprits.

White grubs attract a host of wildlife pests to lawns when populations spike. Raccoons, skunks, crows, and others dig pits, manually probing for the fat grubs. Large scattered pits or holes surrounded by flipped-back sod evidence localized grub infestations drawing animal feeding activity.

Armadillos forage by rooting around in lawns with their long snouts, leaving behind cone-shaped holes 2-3 inches deep. Areas of overturned soil identify armadillos at work. Their digging while feeding on insects damages turfgrass root systems, providing pest entry points.

Groundhogs, also called woodchucks, make golf ball-sized holes leading to their burrows situated along property perimeters. Identifying characteristic groundhog holes and seeing the hefty rodents grazing alerts homeowners to employ repellents or trapping before substantial lawn damage.

The activity of root-feeding skunks often goes undetected until lawn health unexpectedly declines. Skunks excavate small 3-4 inch cone-shaped holes, extracting white grubs and other insect larvae from turf areas. Seeing newly dug pits indicates need for grub control.

Opossums wander lawns at night, eating varied pests harmful to gardens but rarely inflict damage. Any digging is shallow and small. Should damage occur, its random pattern points to opossums. But these beneficial mammals improve turf health by devouring ticks, cockroaches, and other problem insects. No controls are recommended.

Crows pull fallen larval grubs from the ground, leaving holes with fan-shaped dirt patterns behind. But they also peck out and consume seeds when lawns are overseeded, hampering establishment. Identifying crow activity dictates techniques like covering newly seeded areas to limit damage while benefiting from pest control.

Dogs take a toll on lawns through digging, urine burns, feces, and compaction from running. Chewed areas, worn paths, and dead yellow spots identify common dog damage for remediation and training to curb harmful behaviors. Physical barriers like fencing off areas may also be needed.

Cats also negatively impact lawns, digging in soft soils to bury waste. Small depressions with excavated dirt identify feline toilet areas. oFr training redirection, providing dedicated litter spots. Cats' instincts make total lawn avoidance difficult, so vigilance is needed.

Birds like pheasants and wild turkeys scratch and peck at lawns, searching for seeds and insects to eat. Seeing areas of kicked-back grass and leaf litter identifies this disruptive feeding activity. Deterrents can be employed bycovering seeded areas preventing bird damage.

Deer feeding on landscape plants inevitably causes collateral damage to nearby lawns by trampling, bedding down, and compacting. Identifying deer tracks and other signs confirms their presence so repellents, fencing, or other controls can be implemented before extensive damage.

Gophers tunnel extensively below lawns, pulling plant roots down into their underground burrows. Wilting, dying patches indicate their subterranean activity for trap deployment. Conical mounds with plugged holes occasionally appear as they surface. Their damage can destroy entire lawn sections.

Snakes inhabit yards and lawns, secreting themselves beneath mulch, rocks and debris. While harmless to grass, startled homeowners spotting them may demand removal. Identifying hideouts and travel paths allows careful relocation away from recreational spaces where snakes aren't welcome.

Detecting dug-out anthills identifies active ant colonies in your lawn for treatment to prevent mounds from smothering grass in heavily trafficked areas. But recognize that ants aerate soil and feast on other insect pests, playing a role in the landscape's ecosystem beyond merely creating unsightly hills.

Larger livestock like horses, cattle, and sheep trample and graze pasture grasses down to the soil. Hooves also compact soil, reducing oxygen to roots. Observing livestock behavior and movement patterns determines where temporary fencing or reseeding may be needed to let overgrazed areas recover.

Squirrels leave small dug pits around lawns when burying and retrieving nuts. But they also gnaw on tasty turfgrass shoots and tender blades like all rodents. Seeing chewed-off grass clumps beside shallow holes identifies typical squirrel feeding activity. Only extreme cases warrant control measures.

Diagnosing lawn damage from wild or domestic pigs rooting around with their large snouts exposes plots to replanting if extensive. Clipped-off vegetation and flipped-over areas are telltale signs. Fencing, repellents, or exclusion from pig-susceptible sections protects these extremely destructive animals when identified.

Bears foraging under bird feeders leave behind large dug pits scattered across lawns indicative of their presence. They conveniently flip back whole sections of sod to access soil-dwelling grubs and insects. Identifying bear activity should prompt the removal of food attractants so they move on after a short layover.

Careful identification and documentation of all animal pest activity allows you to take appropriate actions for each situation without overreacting. Target controls only where critters pose legitimate risks. Let beneficial species continue their positive lawn contributions unimpeded while safeguarding turfgrasses.

8.5 on Beneficial Insects:

Not all insects inhabiting lawns are pests. Many benign species provide valuable ecosystem services essential for plant health. Learning to identify key beneficial insects allows you to support ideal lawn environments that attract these helpers. Avoid assumed insecticide applications that inadvertently kill valuable allies.

Earthworms continuously recycle organic matter, improving soil nutrients and texture. Seeing their castings on the soil surface evidences this round-the-clock soil amending. Avoid excess synthetic chemicals and nurture ample organic matter to encourage these essential creatures tilling your lawn's underground.

Ground beetles prey on a wide variety of common turfgrass pests. Over 400 species inhabit lawns. Their elusive, nocturnal nature makes them difficult to spot. However, their presence is confirmed by using pitfall traps that capture specimens for identification. Avoid excess lighting that disturbs them.

Antlions in their larval pit-building stage capture all manner of soil-dwelling insects in their underground traps. Adults eat pollen and nectar. Seeing cone-shaped pits evidences successful predation of lawn pests like ants and grubs. Antlions require only moderate soil moisture to thrive.

Centipedes reside under plant debris and leaf litter, emerging at night to ambush soft-bodied lawn pests. The small, many-legged creatures kill more prey than they can eat. While creepy looking to some homeowners, recognize centipedes' role in controlling populations of detrimental insects and worms harmful to turfgrass.

Clover mites prey on hundreds of mite and insect species that damage lawns, but the tiny red specks are rarely noticed. Their beneficial predation prevents pest mite species from reaching epidemic levels. Avoiding broad-spectrum insecticide applications allows clover mites' food source to persist so they stick around.

Golden glow beetles are a variety of lightning bugs whose larvae live underground, preying on grubs, cutworms, and other lawn-damaging insect larvae.Ttheir summer nighttime light show signals a successful biocontrol of subsurface pests by these beneficial insects identifiable from other species by their signature glow color.

Soldier beetles are aptly named for their aggressive predatory feeding on aphids, caterpillars, beetle larvae, grasshopper eggs, and other lawn and garden pests. Adults fly in seeking pollen sources. Seeing these black and orange beneficial insects signals an active, healthy lawn ecosystem.

Green lacewings are attracted to lawns and gardens by ample nectar sources where the delicate-looking adults lay eggs. Once voracious larvae hatch, they consume soft-bodied insects like aphids, mealybugs, scales, and spider mites, damaging plants. Lacewings require only insecticides harmless to them for optimal natural pest control.

Lady beetles, also called ladybugs, are welcomed in lawns where both their larvae and adults feed on destructive soft-bodied insects and mites. A single ladybug may eat over 50 aphids daily. Avoid pesticides, so this colorful beneficial insect controls pests naturally. Plant pollen and nectar plants to attract and retain them.

Ground beetle larvae live in lawns' thatch layer, preying on slugs, snails, cutworms, and other insects that can damage turfgrass. The inch-long larvae are gray or brown with large jaws for efficiently dispatching prey several times their size. Seeing them when aerate-dethatching signals effective natural pest control below. Predatory mites inhabit lawns, feeding on pest mites, thrips, and other small insects. They form no webs and are hard to spot without magnification. But their presence keeps destructive spider mites under control. Avoiding miticides protects these microscopic beneficial mites.

Ground beetle adults actively pursue surface-dwelling pests like slugs and snails. Metallic green or reddish colors distinguish their quick-moving half-inch bodies. Seeing them dash about at night signals effective pest control patrols taking place after sundown.

Fireflies, also called lightning bugs, fill summer evenings with their signature glow. But by day, their larvae live underground, preying on soil-dwelling insects. The larvae have hearty appetites, feeding on pests like slugs, snails, beetles, and worms. Their flashy shows reveal robust beneficial larvae populations.

Hoverflies are sometimes mistaken for bees, but they cause no harm. Adults feed on pollen while their larvae ravenously consume aphids, caterpillars, and other soft plant-sucking insects in lawns and landscapes. Spotting them indicates they are laying eggs and controlling pests naturally.

Minute pirate bugs live up to their ferocious name, feeding on a variety of small insects and mites which damage plants. Adults often go unnoticed due to their tiny size, but their active hunting keeps potential lawn pests like thrips, aphids, and spider mites in check as part of the diverse beneficial insect community.

Big-eyed bugs get their name from their enlarged bulging eyes, which give them superb vision for hunting insect eggs, aphids, mites, and newly hatched caterpillars in turfgrass. Though only 1/10 inch long, they eat prey much larger than themselves, providing key natural pest control.

Assassin bugs are aptly named for their effective hunting of a wide range of insects attacking lawns and gardens. Also called wheel bugs for their cog-shaped nymphs, they inject immobilizing enzymes into their prey. Seeing them demonstrates successful biocontrol of problem pests in your landscape.

Parasitic wasps prey on a diverse array of insects in lawns. The adult wasp lays its eggs inside host insects. When the eggs hatch, the larvae devour their host from within. Look for caterpillars and insect larvae with white wasp cocoons attached to their bodies, a clear sign of parasitism.

Mealybug destroyers prey in great numbers on lawn and garden pests like mealybugs, aphids, and Japanese beetle larvae. The tan ladybugs with black spots are welcome sights, as adults and larvae feed on target prey. Their presence indicates effective natural pest control already established.

Spiders residing in lawns provide exceptional insect control. Many build barely visible webs to trap aerial prey like mosquitoes, flies, and leafhoppers that damage turfgrass. Seeing webbing spanning lawn plants signals beneficial predators at work controlling airborne pests.

With careful observation and identification, you may find an array of surprising natural pest control allies already patrolling your lawn. Avoid disrupting them with excess pesticide applications. Instead, nurture conditions through thoughtful organic practices that attract and sustain this hidden army.

8.6 on Integrated Pest Management:

Integrated Pest Management (IPM) is a smart, environmentally responsible approach to controlling lawn pests. Rather than relying solely on pesticides, IPM utilizes a combination of methods to prevent and manage pest problems while minimizing risks. Employing IPM requires understanding pest biology and habits, proper lawn maintenance, monitoring for early detection, and implementing a combination of physical, cultural, biologica,l and chemical controls.

The key to successful IPM is prevention. The first line of defense is to maintain a healthy, vigorous lawn. Many pests attack stressed, unhealthy grass. Proper mowing, irrigation, fertilization, and soil preparation promote dense, resilient turf. Select pest-resistant grass varieties when establishing a new lawn. Routinely inspect your lawn to spot pests early when they are easiest to control. Identify problem areas and understand pest life cycles. Focus on improving these vulnerable zones.

Once pests are detected, a variety of low-risk control methods can be implemented. Physical controls like hand-picking weeds, traps, barriers, and nest removal disrupt pest life cycles. Biological controls utilize natural predators, parasites, or disease organisms to manage pests. Beneficial nematodes attack soil-dwelling insects. Bacillus thuringiensis (Bt) bacteria kill caterpillar, but are safe for mammals. Natural predators like ladybugs, lacewings, and birds can be attracted to habitat plants.

Cultural practices modify the lawn environment to suppress pests. Adjust mowing height, watering, and fertilizer to favor grass growth over weeds. Thatch removal and aeration alleviate soil compaction and stress. Alternating mowing direction prevents rutting patterns that attract pests. Overseeding crowds out space for weed seeds to germinate. Corn gluten meal provides natural pre-emergent weed control.

When pest damage exceeds acceptable thresholds despite preventative IPM tactics, selective spot treatments with least-toxic pesticides may be warranted. Micro-applications target individual weeds or affected areas, reducing overall chemical usage. Botanical derivatives, soaps, and oils are lower-risk options. Granular iron phosphate baits control snails and slugs. Systemic herbicides target root systems while avoiding pollinators. Always follow label directions and safety precautions when using any pesticide.

An integrative IPM plan should combine multiple strategies for each pest issue. Crabgrass might be tackled through pre-emergent corn gluten application, hand-weeding young sprouts, spot-spraying herbicides on clumps, and overseeding in fall to crowd it out long-term. Grubs could be controlled by applying beneficial nematodes, adjusting watering to reduce stress, aerating for better beneficial nematode penetration, and limiting spot applications of grub killer once thresholds are exceeded.

Implementing IPM requires diligent monitoring through regular lawn inspections. Keep records detailing pest levels, conditions favoring pests, habitat improvements, control methods applied, and effectiveness. Use this data to evaluate and tweak your IPM plan year after year. Be patient, as it may take multiple seasons to successfully transition from routine pesticide use to proactive prevention. But the payoff is substantial, creating a vibrant lawn ecosystem with fewer pests naturally and less reliance on chemicals.

IPM does permit judicious pesticide use, but only after preventative measures fail to provide adequate control. Any products applied should target the specific pest and life stage while minimizing environmental impact. Prioritize least toxic choices and micro-applications over broadcast spraying. Understand pesticide families and modes of action to avoid overuse or resistance. Always follow safety precautions and label directions.

An IPM approach requires more attentive management than blanket chemical applications. However, the investment pays dividends through reduced pest pressure over time. You gain a thorough understanding of your landscape's challenges and interactions. A thoughtfully designed IPM plan tailored to your lawn and pests keeps your grass healthy and lush while protecting the broader environment. And you can enjoy your yard knowing it reflects your own environmental values. A comprehensive IPM program should address the full spectrum of potential lawn pests. Common weed types each require specific prevention and control methods. Annual weeds like crabgrass and spurge reproduce by seed, so pre-emergent corn gluten applications in early spring can inhibit development. Hand-pull young annuals before they mature and spread seeds. Broadleaf perennials like dandelions and clover propagate through roots and rhizomes, making systemic herbicides more effective. Grassy perennials, including nimblewill, must be continually dug out and smothered or spotted with glyphosate.

Insects damaging lawns range from subsurface pests like grubs to aboveground chinch bugs and billbugs. Beneficial nematodes control grub larvae before they feed on grass roots. Parasitic wasps help suppress chinch bugs. Adjusting fertilizer timing and watering reduces environmental stress favorable to billbugs. Scout for early signs of insect activity, like brown patches or dying grass. Only apply insecticides like Bacillus thuringiensis when substantial damage is seen. Always follow label instructions carefully.

Disease issues mainly arise from excessive moisture. Improve drainage and reduce irrigation to dry out the lawn. Rake thatch buildup to improve ai flow. Space out sprinklers to allow faster drying. Apply corn gluten meal in the fall to suppress disease spores. Fungicides should be a last resort for serious outbreaks. Excessive disease problems may indicate unsuitable grass varieties for your climate. Consider resistant cultivars when renovating.

Animal pests like moles burrow and tunnel through lawns, disrupting roots and foundations. Limit their food source by controlling grubs and insects with beneficial nematodes. Use vibration devices or repellents to deter tunneling. Fill in tunnels and tamp down runs to discourage reuse. Block entry holes with hardware cloth or wire mesh. Be patient, as successful animal control takes time and persistence.

A critical but often overlooked part of IPM is enhancing natural biological controls. Lady beetles, green lacewings, praying mantises, birds, and bats all help suppress pests. Avoid broad-spectrum pesticides that inadvertently kill these beneficials. Plant native flowers and shrubs to provide pollen, nectar, and shelter for natural predators. Install bat houses and bird feeders to encourage presence. Provide bee blocks, butterfly houses, and insect hotels. A healthy ecosystem supports a diversity of helpful organisms to reduce pests naturally.

Like any ecological system, lawns constantly evolve. The pests, diseases, and environmental conditions impacting a lawn will change over time. An effective IPM plan must be continually evaluated and updated to address emerging challenges. Review records over the seasons to identify patterns and especially problematic areas. Certain sections may be chronically afflicted with disease, indicating a drainage issue or a need to alter grass species. Some pests may regularly appear at certain times, allowing you to plan preventative tactics in advance. Make adjustments annually based on past results.

There is no definitive template for a lawn IPM plan. Each landscape has a unique mix of pests, conditions, and homeowner goals. Be willing to experiment to find the optimal combination of prevention, control methods, and acceptable damage thresholds for your yard. Vary the timing of beneficial nematode application or pre-emergent weed control. Test different natural herbicides. Add flowering plants to encourage beneficials. IPM requires actively shaping your lawn ecosystem to suppress pests naturally.

Embracing IPM philosophy for lawn care represents a fundamental shift from reactive pesticide use to proactive prevention and natural control. It requires diligent effort over multiple seasons to transition your landscape successfully. But the lasting rewards are substantial, including reduced pest pressure, lower maintenance, enhanced biodiversity and wildlife habitat, protection of pollinators, and filtered runoff into waterways. Your lawn becomes part of the broader ecosystem. Utilizing IPM creates a vibrant, resilient outdoor space for you and your community to enjoy.

Jamie Tukey

Closing Remarks:

As we reach the end of our lawn care journey together, I hope this book has provided you with a comprehensive overview and valuable insights into caring for your landscape. A beautiful, thriving lawn is within your grasp, but achieving it requires knowledge, proper techniques, and diligent care across the seasons. Consider this book your guidebook - a resource to reference again and again as you cultivate the lush, vibrant lawn of your dreams.

Caring for a lawn sustainably is an ongoing process of learning and fine-tuning. Do not be discouraged if your lawn does not transform overnight. Creating an ecological oasis takes patience and persistence. Follow the core practices outlined here and adapt them year after year based on your lawn's unique needs. See challenges like pests, weeds, and bare spots as opportunities to improve your skills. A stunning landscape is cultivated gradually through care and attention over time.

I hope the knowledge gained from this book empowers you to take an active role in your lawn's health. Understand how proper mowing, watering, fertilizing, and soil care create the foundation for success. Implement organic practices to nurture the living ecosystem beneath your feet. Be proactive against pests through integrated solutions. Discover the satisfaction of growing thick, green grass while also protecting the environment. May this book open your eyes to see your lawn as part of something greater - your local ecology and global community.

As a final reminder - take joy in the process! Do not view lawn care solely as a chore. Find opportunities to relax and decompress as you work amidst nature. The fresh air, sunshine, and scents of soil and grass have restorative effects on the body and mind. Share the experience by gardening with family, friends, or neighbors. Take pride as your hard work transforms bare dirt into a welcoming green oasis for the community. And pause to appreciate the beauty around you - birds bathing in sprinklers, butterflies dancing above blooms, and children laughing as they play in the grass.

Thank you for allowing me to be a part of your lawn care journey. I wish you the very best as you cultivate a beautiful, sustainable landscape. May your lawn become a vibrant, healthy ecosystem and cherished gathering space for years to come. Now step outside, grab your tools, and let's grow something amazing together.